Nothing Like Ri
New ~~~~~~~
Memoirs of a Woman Outfitter in Montana

by

Mary Faith Hoeffner

Compiled by Brad Hansen

THIS IS MY STORY AS I REMEMBER

Oh, these darn horses will be the death of me yet! I was sitting on my buckskin horse, Badger, when he suddenly dropped to his knees and rolled to the side, his back was itching. I kicked him and slid out from under him as he stood up, but didn't realize my foot was caught in the stirrup. My foot was on his back, leaving me underneath. Not wanting to be drug across the pasture, I yelled to Jeff at the top of my lungs to catch the horse before he decided to run. Thank God for Jeff, because a cowboy's worst nightmare is being drug by their horse.

Friends tell me I should write a book. I am not sure about that, but guess I better "get er done." My kids all loved the mountains. Other families go to Disneyworld, etc., but my family enjoyed the mountains and still does.

They say every woman needs a good man, a good horse, and a good dog. Guess I've had them all.

I am not an authority on outfitting, wilderness, horse breaking, or even raising a family. But I have lived the life and rode the miles. This is my story, my memoir!

-Mary Faith Hoeffner
Lincoln, Montana, October 2014

CONTENTS

INTRODUCTION

I first met Mary Faith during the fall of 2014 at her ranch in Lincoln, Montana. My good friend, Jim Stein, arranged the meeting, along with her son Jeff Hoeffner and his wife Marie. The plan was to record a few of Mary Faith's adventures. As Jim and I drove over the Continental Divide, he pointed out the location on Flesher Pass where Mary Faith had once slid her pickup off the road and down a cliff. As we dropped into Lincoln and crossed the Big Blackfoot River, Jim mentioned that Mary Faith had once lost her horses to the river when its banks filled with poison from an upstream mine. It was around the same time, he said, that her dad and stepmother had been in a gun fight up Alice Creek. "Geez," I thought. "Who is this lady?"

When we arrived at the ranch house, Mary Faith was nowhere to be found. On the front door was a note. "Gone Riding Deer Lodge." Jim laughed and said we might as well get comfortable because Mary Faith could be awhile. Deer Lodge is 70 miles from Lincoln. A few minutes later, however, Mary Faith appeared across the meadow. She was driving a golf cart that looked like it had spent more time off road than most ATVs. I looked at Jim and said, "I guess the note is old." At 82 years, her eyes were bright and she moved on her feet like she was 35. She shook my hand and asked if I'd like to meet her horses.

Mary Faith loved horses. Her adventures always involved a horse. From her teenage and college years as a trick rider and member of the Montana State College Rodeo Team, to her adult life as an outfitter, Mary Faith mastered the art of horsemanship. Those who knew her best said she was happiest on a horse in the backcountry. It's not surprising that she took up outfitting. For twenty years Mary Faith operated K Lazy Three Outfitters with her husband Kenny and their five children. When Kenny passed away in January 1989, she operated the business with her son, Jeff, for another ten seasons.

As one of Montana's first women outfitters, she was a pioneer. She bucked (no pun intended) the stereotype that outfitting was solely a man's game, and proved that a woman could guide and manage camp just as well as anybody. She had her fair share of trials and navigated them with an optimism we can all envy. She rode and guided and cooked and raised a family. And when grizzlies raided the meat poles in camp at night, she held the lantern while Kenny fired at the sound of cow bells running down the trail in the dark.

Montana's Bob Marshall and Scapegoat Wildernesses were the backdrop for many of her adventures, including those that left their mark! A concussion, a broken right leg, a broken left leg, a broken knee cap. For better or worse, Mary Faith got to know the inside of the Mercy Flight helicopter. One of her broken legs left her stranded on top of a mountain in below zero temperatures and deep snow. Unable to walk, Mary Faith made a shelter to block the wind and used her hunting knife to hollow out a nearby log. Always resourceful, she used her hunting license and a cigarette lighter she found in her coat to build a fire in the hollow of the log and stay alive until help arrived. Mary Faith lived by the maxim (which was framed and hung on a wall in her ranch house): "Life should not be a journey to the grave with the intention of arriving safely in a pretty and well preserved body, but rather to skid in broadside in a cloud of smoke, thoroughly used up, totally worn out, and loudly proclaiming "Wow! What a Ride!"

Checking out in a hospital or long-term care facility was never in the cards for Mary Faith. Each time the doctors said she wouldn't make it out, she did. They sent her to rehab and she ran away. It took three police cars and an ambulance to track her down, and when they found her she argued that "she was a citizen and had rights, god damnit." She made it clear she wasn't going back to rehab, and so her children moved her back into the ranch house in Lincoln. She spent two months giving rides to visitors on the beat-up golf cart and tending to her horses. When she couldn't drive any longer, or get out to see her horses, her family brought them to her. Outside her bedroom window she watched the leaves turn and her favorite buckskin Badger nibble yellow grass in the meadow. On her ranch, in the shadow of the wilderness, Mary Faith took her last breath. She lived and died on her own terms, a true pioneer woman.

At the funeral, the church was filled to overflowing with outfitters, friends, and former clients. At the cemetery, her children had the horses ready. As the family rode out together there was one horse without a rider. The buckskin wore Mary Faith's hat and saddle. Several hundred people gathered at Lincoln High School afterwards. They shook hands and sang campfire songs. Everyone had a story to share. This book is Mary Faith's story, in her own words. I hope you enjoy it as much as I have!

Brad Hansen,
Helena, Montana, July 2017

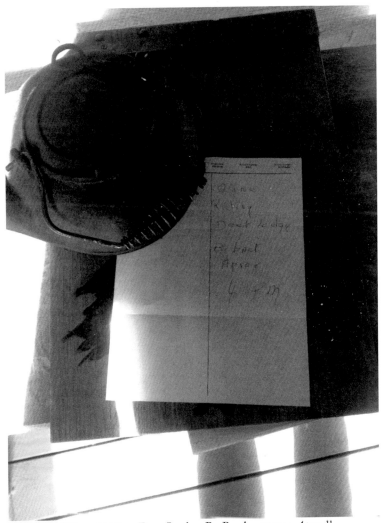

"Gone Riding Deer Lodge, Be Back approx. 4pm."

Mary Faith and Kenneth R. Hoeffner's Children

Judy, Jeff, Mary Faith, Jerrie, Jackie, and Penny Jo, at the wedding of granddaughter Desiree Downing, 2013.

v

1 THE FAIRFIELD YEARS

We raised frying chickens each year, and since I was the oldest, I got to chop off their heads and watch them jump around squirting blood everywhere. —Mary Faith Hoeffner

I was born April 24, 1932, in Great Falls, Montana, the first of five children born to L. Kenneth and Faith Mills McLean. I had two sisters, Nancy and JoAnne and two brothers, Barry Stephen and Kenny. We lived on Graves Lane, east of Fairfield, Montana. Graves Lane was named for Lemuel Graves who homesteaded there in 1900. My grandmother, Ada McLean, her brothers, Barney and Bill, and family friend Beverly Graves, all came from Grangeville, Idaho. Mom and dad's first home was a granary on grandpa McLean's farm. Times were tough during the depression years of the 1930s, but families were close. They worked together and shared what they could.

The Graves family was originally from Kentucky by way of Grangeville, Idaho, where Franch McLean, a local businessman, met Ada. We all called Ada "Banjo," which was started by an older cousin. She was a staunch Democrat and Catholic who was very proud to have shook the hand of John F. Kennedy. Mom's family lived in Simms, Montana, at the time she and dad met. I was born on dad's birthday and JoAnne, my sister, was born on Mom's birthday, May 12, 1933. Both of my sisters, JoAnne and Nancy were born in Great Falls, but we all grew up on the Fairfield Homestead. Our family moved to Fairfield, Montana, where Grandpa McLean had been appointed postmaster with Banjo his assistant. Dad started a coal delivery business on the side and delivered mail part time on the Greenfield Route east of Fairfield. He was a very busy man.

Dad had two sisters, Bea Crabtree and Mary Henderson, who lived in Simms and Fairfield. We had a lot of family gatherings at Christmas, Easter, and on birthdays, and we had picnics with our cousins and family. Banjo would sometimes have us over on Fridays, or for waffles after church on Sunday. The Mills family lived in Fairfield in a very nice house. Grandma Mills played the piano beautifully and tried to teach us girls to play, but we were more interested in horses and outdoor stuff.

Ada "Banjo" McLean and Frank McLean (Mary Faith's great-grandfather) in Salem, Oregon.

Mary Edna Faith Mills McLean and L. Kenneth McLean with their children Nancy, Mary Faith, and JoAnne, ca. 1938.

"New Cowboy Outfits" left to right: Nancy McLean, Mary Faith McLean, JoAnne McLean, Kenny McLean, and Ray and Ron Mills (cousins), ca. 1942.

Original photo damaged in Montana Flood of 1964.
Digital photo restoration by Mark McLean 1997.

Mary Edna Faith Mills, mother of Mary Faith Hoeffner, ca. 1915.

On the Fourth of July the McLean sisters would all dress up for the parade. JoAnne, "the lady" wore a black dress, hat, and parasol. Nancy wore a red, white, and blue dress and hat. Me in a black and white cowgirl outfit with chaps and riding a pony! Leave it to mom, she always put together nice outfits for us to wear. Me and JoAnne sang "Ragtime Cowboy Joe" at the community benefit hall. Mom and dad were wonderful dancers. Us girls danced with dad to learn how.

Faith Edna Mills and L. Kenneth McLean, ca. 1930s.

Soon, homestead land opened west of Fairfield. Dad had always wanted to get back to farming and raising livestock, so he and mom filed on a homestead; 160 acres for each of them. Uncle John and aunt Bea Crabtree moved from Simms and did the same, a few miles to the west of us. It was all open grassland then, so we started from scratch.

We moved our house from Fairfield to the homestead 8 miles west of town and planted seven rows of trees for a shelterbelt. I know there were seven rows because I helped plant them. It later turned out that we had the best shelterbelt in the area. We planted a yard and garden and dad plowed the land to begin farming with his new Case tractor. There were chickens, a milk cow, and horses. We raised frying chickens each year, and since I was the oldest I got to chop off their heads and watch them jump around squirting blood everywhere. Mom made the best fried chicken in a cast iron skillet. Mom and dad were both ambitious and hardworking people; us kids loved them.

Dad always liked horses and taught us girls how to ride and take care of them. We had a pigpen and bum lambs that dad got free from the Lowery Ranch. Us kids fed them each morning before school and at night using rubber nipples and pop bottles. We had Herford calves for 4H, which we had to teach to lead. They would run away with us until they learned. We sold them at the fair. One year I raised pigs, a belted Hampshire sow and ten little piglets. I won some prizes and made money to ride the Ferris wheel and roller coaster and play games. What a great time for us girls. We slept in the back of the pickup during the fair.

Back to the garden. We had a big white work horse named Lobo, which dad used to cultivate the potatoes. I rode him to make sure he didn't step on anything. If he did, I was in trouble. We girls rode all over the prairie, which was open range at the time, no fences. Since cousin Audrey Crabtree lived a few miles to the west, we frequently rode together and in the big coulee, which had a small stream. Us girls' other job was to bring the milk cows home in the evening after school. We didn't come home without them. We knew where they usually hung out.

Mary Faith (eight years old) riding Major (one year old) near Fairfield, Montana, ca. 1930s.

Sometimes we rode the milk cows out of the barn and did all the other fun stuff kids did on a farm. Our games were hide and seek in the shelterbelt in summer time, and fox and geese in winter. My very first horse, if I remember, was an old sorrel mare named Pet. It was hard telling how old she was! I had another small paint Shetland named Major, but he bucked me off and broke my arm, so dad traded him for a gray mare named Stranger. She was bred to a paint. She had a colt, but it was not a paint. He was gray with one glass eye; we named him Bucko. Bucko turned out to be my trick riding horse. I rode him Labor Day weekend in Great Falls and at Augusta in the first Montana high school rodeo. I had three tricks I could do. Zana Zumwalt taught me the Russian Drag, Roman Stand, and One Foot Stand. Then our sheepherder, an old Irish guy named Shorty, went on a big drunk and bought me a bay thoroughbred named Pal. He could run!

JoAnne needed a horse too, so dad bought her a gray Hamilton mare she named Trixie. We rode her home from Simms and got caught up in some wire; what a ride, no one hurt! Unfortunately, Pal and JoAnne's horse Trixie got into some poison oats, treated for planting. Dad found them dead at the sheep shed. We were all broken hearted that day! I had never seen dad so upset. Later a family friend, Jim Hughes, knew a horse trader in Shelby. Dad bought a bay mare named Sugar and a palomino stallion, Sonny. I trick rode on him, but he became JoAnne's horse and we both barrel raced him. Sugar had a wonderful colt we named Sassy that Jackie and I rode in barrel races in Lincoln, Montana. We always had horses. Dad and us kids loved them. I remember Dad and I riding the horses to pasture in Simms. Dad's horse was Fox, who he was very proud of. On the way, Fox spooked and bucked Dad off. Boy, I was afraid he was hurt, tore his shirt, but he got back on and away we went.

Dad liked to try new crops so he planted sugar beets one year and hired a group of Mexicans to harvest them. Dad planted hay peas and flax one year also. We had two hundred sheep, which us kids herded during the summer in the big coulee to keep them out of the crops. I remember sheep shearing time and the big wool bags, which we got into to tramp down the bundles of wool. We came out very oily and with a few ticks on us, but it was fun! Dad built a sheep shed from woven wool and flax straw. It was located in the open range area in the big coulee and had a corral and pens to use at lambing time. The only trouble was the sheep liked to eat the flax straw and the roof leaked, but it worked well enough. I got to do lots of "boy" things with dad as the oldest girl. I drove the tractor, drove the hay stacker team, and learned to be careful or the cable would break. I loved it all.

My brothers, Stephen and Kenny, were born at the Fairfield homestead. I wanted to name my brother Barry Stephen, but we decided the initials B.S. weren't any good, so he became Stephen Barry. On the Fourth of July, our families went to Benchmark, Montana, many times to camp and fish. We caught our first fish there, and always had some firecrackers. We slept in a big tent and later dad and uncle Clarence built a tent frame with a floor and a place for a stove and door to put the tent on. I remember what fun it was for us kids riding in the back of the pickup with the camping gear to the mountains to camp.

Mary Faith and Bucko practicing at the Augusta Ranch, ca. 1930s.

Stephen Barry, L. Kenneth, and Kenny McLean, ca. 1940s.

2 THE AUGUSTA YEARS

Indian paintbrush, buttercups, Johnny jump-ups, glacier lilies (one of the first as snow leaves), wild geraniums, wild onion, elephant heads, and monkey flowers in damp draws, arrow-leaf balsam root (large yellow flowers), vines, fireweed, columbine. Mushrooms —different types and shapes. New signs of life everywhere. New colts, baby deer, elk calves, grouse, or you might see a bear or moose with a calf! Air is fresh. New tracks on the trail — only the sound of horse shoes striking the rock or creaking of leather. —Mary Faith Hoeffner

In 1948 dad met Fred Romaine at a livestock sale in Great Falls. Dad bought some registered Herford cattle from him and they later became partners in raising Polled Herefords. They bought a 5,000-acre ranch west of Augusta known as the Sawtooth Herford Ranch, where we raised and sold registered bulls. Dad sold the homestead at Fairfield and got ready to move. JoAnne, Nancy, me, and cousin Audrey rode the 30 miles herding our livestock, and camped one night on the ride to the new ranch. There was farming machinery, household goods, etc., to be moved so it took several trips. It was a wonderful ranch where we were all happy and busy with ranch work. There were two streams bordering the hay land: Little Willow Creek and Big Willow Creek. I was like the oldest boy working with dad, and I helped the men put up hay that summer. I drove Toots and Topsy to rake hay with a dump rake. We also moved hay on the Sun River Game Range. Kenny, Stephen, JoAnne, Nancy, and mom were all busy too.

There were rodeos and dances in Augusta. Me and my sisters became quite the rodeo girls. Our family was involved in bringing the first high school rodeo to Montana in 1950 at Augusta. I won first place in barrel racing that year. JoAnne was voted rodeo queen on her horse Sonny. She and I barrel raced and did the cow cutting competition. I also rode Doug Deer's cutting horse. Dad later bought a dun-colored stallion from Deer named Coke, and I used him as a turn back horse in cow cutting competitions. Nancy later won the all-around cowgirl on Post Tosties, a great cutting horse that dad bought in Denver at the livestock show. Dad loved horses and going to the

Denver stock show, where he also bought Colonel, a beautiful sorrel quarter horse, which he rode for many years.

What happened to me? Well, after graduating high school I went to Montana State College in Bozeman for a year to rodeo, but I missed home. I also missed Kenny Hoeffner, a handsome ranch boy who was my high school beau. The Hoeffner family owned a ranch farther up Willow Creek from our place. We began dating sometime in high school and married in 1952. Kenny joined the United States Air Force and was stationed in Denver, Colorado, so mom, dad, Kenny, Stephen, and Kenny's mother, Berdie, drove to Denver for Kenny and me to be married. A few months later Kenny and his B-29 bomber crew were transferred to Okinawa to fly in the Korean War. I stayed home where Jackie was born in Choteau, Montana. JoAnne and Nancy lived at home and did barrel racing and cutting horse competitions in rodeos. Jackie was spoiled rotten with all the aunts, uncles, and grandparents at the ranch. She and I had one of the three bedrooms upstairs in the ranch house until Kenny was reassigned to Mt. Home, Idaho, where we joined him until he finished his enlistment. That's where Jerrie was born, a tiny cute little girl. We lived in a 27-foot trailer near the air force base, with no bath or toilet. It wasn't too bad though. Good neighbors, all young and in the same boat. We were broke most of the time since servicemen's pay wasn't much. We played Pinochle and horseshoes together. Good hunting and fishing. We liked Idaho but wanted to get back to the ranch at Augusta.

When we finally returned to Augusta, we lived in a bunkhouse for a year until dad moved the old post office building from Fairfield to put together a house for us. Kenny went to work for dad when Judy was born. I was terribly busy with my three little girls. We helped him remodel it and moved in. We had a big Thanksgiving dinner at our house that year. Banjo and grandpa, Berdie and John Hoeffner, and all of my family came.

Kenny worked for dad only about a year. Kenny and dad had different ideas about the ranch. The last straw for Kenny was when dad brought in sheep. We later left the ranch and moved our little family to a house east of Augusta on the Sun River. Kenny worked for Bruce Cornell tending bar for a while, and we later moved to Fairfield, where he sold farm machinery. Kenny was a good salesman and enjoyed people. I planted a big garden and potato patch across the street from the Catholic church. Since Banjo, grandma McLean and aunt Peggy lived nearby, we went to church with them. Because of my love for the outdoors and working with livestock, I was determined to live on a ranch and not be a city girl. Soon after, mom and dad got a divorce and dad remarried Marion Alfson, sold the ranch and bought a house in Great Falls as well as cabins on Roger's Pass. They were called the Evergreen Cabins.

Mary Faith McLean competing as a member of the Montana State College Rodeo Team. Spike Van Cleve (photo right) judging, ca. 1950s.

Mary Faith Hoeffner and her oldest daughter Jackie on Post Tosties at the Augusta Ranch, ca. 1950s.

Newlyweds Kenny and Mary Faith Hoeffner with Mary Faith's parents in Denver, Colorado, 1952.

*John and Alberta (Berdie) Hoeffner (Kenny's parent's) at the wedding of their
son Russell Hoeffner and his wife Kris.*

Kenny Hoeffner, United States Airforce, B-29 Gunner.

3 THE LINCOLN RANCH

We had twenty cows of our own and got an FHA loan for another fifty and lease pasture and hay land. Dad said, "You can't make a living in Lincoln raising cattle. Winters are too long." You know, he was right. – Mary Faith Hoeffner.

On Father's Day 1955, we went to Lincoln, Montana, for a picnic with Banjo, aunt Mary, and uncle Clarence at their beautiful 160-acre farm. Kenny and I immediately fell in love with it, so in 1959, we bought our little dream ranch from aunt Mary and uncle Clarence. We moved to Lincoln with our three little girls, Jackie, Jerrie, and Judy to a house with no bathroom, a wood cook stove, and one heating stove in the living room. It was simple, but we were happy. The house was really set up as a log cabin, which was built in 1920. The house consisted of a large 16-by-20 foot log living room, one bedroom, and kitchen with walls filled with sawdust for insulation. Logs were six to a side. Sod roof with a gable built over it. I loved it, we were happy. No bathroom, just a path to the outhouse and a small corner off the kitchen we used as a toilet. It took lots of wood to keep the wood cook stove and two tin heaters going, seemed like we were out of wood and money all the time!

The first year we calved without a barn. We had snow, and cold, and pine needle abortion. We lost many calves. Dad came and was happy to help. Kenny's younger brother, Russell Hoeffner, also helped with calving and putting up wood and hay for the winter. Sometimes we ran out of wood, hay, and groceries that winter. I also became pregnant with Penny Jo, our fourth daughter. She was born July 7, 1960. My dad came to Lincoln that winter and said, "You have to have a bathroom," so he and a friend and Kenny added a bathroom and utility room.

The spring I was pregnant with Penny Jo I rode a little and drove the truck when we moved cows to summer pasture. There were no fences in that area, so cows were scattered all over the place. Kenny's older brother, Ed, came to help. No pay for Ed, just food and a place to sleep. He and Kenny put up hay on the Sucker Creek Ranch and

Doc Andes place. We moved the cows out there for fall pasture and hauled the hay home for winter feed. It seems like the tractor was always broke down. I raked hay with a baby on my lap, round and round the hay field.

Kenny was so capable and ambitious that he bought a D6 Cat to skid logs together with Don Martin. He and Anne Martin were our good friends along with Ruth and Art Glaze. We shared many cups of coffee together with them to sort things out. Jackie started first grade that fall with Jerrie and Judy to follow. I remember Jackie was in first grade and we drove her to school. There was no school bus. I remember her saying "Can't I have a candy bar for lunch?" She probably had pancakes or sandwiches in her pack. I remember saying, "Jackie, we are about to lose the ranch, no candy bars!"

Judy, Jerrie, and Jackie Hoeffner, ca. 1960s

Kenny Hoeffner at the Lincoln Ranch, ca. 1950s.

Making a Go at It

We wanted a ranch, but oh the cold and snow. We were in the cattle business, but little did we know about the long winters in Lincoln. Come spring, we were calving a bunch of cows. We lost calves to pine needle abortion. Lots of sick calves in the house. Don't think we ever got over losing the calves. They are all so cute. But we were happy. We had the family, horses, and cows, but no barn. So, Kenny and friends built a barn down by the spring with rough lumber and chain saws. It's still standing to this day, and very useable. Kenny built a tack room and stalls. Kenny was also a tree faller (one of the best!) for the county. He could do just about anything.

We had no idea how much hay it would take for the winter or how much wood we'd need. It was a challenge. In the meantime, my dad acquired an outfitting camp up on Crow Creek in the mountains near Lincoln, so Kenny began guiding hunters for him.

I became pregnant again and on November 7, 1961, our one son, Jeff, was born. I remember well because the doctor came to my room at St. Pete's Hospital to tell me my husband was on the next floor down with broken ribs and bruises from rolling a D6 cat off Stemple Pass. Wow, what to do! A baby boy and four little girls. Luckily, dad came to the hospital and took Kenny, me, and baby Jeff to the ranch and took care of us and fed the livestock. Neighbors came every evening at 5:00 pm with a dish for supper. What wonderful neighbors. We were grateful. What a wonderful dad.

My daughters Jackie and Jerrie were in girls drill team with their horses. Jerrie was seven years old and rode her horse Spooks; Jackie rode Sassy. The drill team was called "The Purple Sage Riders." A lady from Lincoln directed them. The girls often rode many of Jean Youdarian's dude horses. It was a beautiful drill team made up of all local girls. They rode in Lincoln and Helmville. Kenny and I were very active in the rodeo club and I remember carrying flags on Sassy. We painted the bucking shoots with white paint.

Lots of PTA and VFW meetings for me, basket socials, basketball games, and proms. Judy was prom queen in Augusta, with her dress from Salvation Army! It was so pretty. Jeff and Penny Jo were in basketball and track meets, football also for Jeff. More proms and Christmas programs. We drove the kids to school in Lincoln. I became great friends with Ruth Glaze. We had coffee together after driving kids to school for many years.

My children all went to grade school in Lincoln and high school in Augusta. When they were old enough to play on the teams they would board in Augusta during the week and come home on weekends. A home game was 60 miles away. An away game was over 100 miles. Jackie and Jerrie were both cheerleaders and Judy played basketball and cheered. Penny Jo played basketball and cheered as well. She was tough! Jeff played football and basketball.

Jackie and Mary Faith riding Comanche at the Lincoln Ranch with two of Mary Faith's dogs in the background.

Mary Faith and Kenny Hoeffner's horses grazing along the Rocky Mountain Front as winter melts into spring.

Summers on the Ranch

Springtime – wildflowers start popping up –crocus, buttercup and glacier lilies, Johnny jumpups. We hired a rancher to level our front field for more hay and better irrigation. We planted the field with first year oats and hay. Beautiful crops! Water in the ditch about middle April or first of May. Water comes into our Lincoln ranch from the Blackfoot River. Our water rights date back to 1888. What a great feeling when water comes in! Dig out the dams and start irrigating the fields. Harrow the fields and put on fertilizer. Hope it grows, always need hay! Plant my garden! I always loved my garden with potatoes, lots of rutabaga (even raised purple potatoes) carrots, beets, lettuce and wonderful cabbage, onions and squash, and maybe tomatoes on the south side of the house.

Branding was always an exciting time. We had at one time fifty cows. Always more cowboys than cows! Haying started about the 15th of July. Swath, rake, and bale then stack in the barn. Then pack some of the hay down the trail to camp. We sold certified hay, no weeds.

Trucking Cattle

We also trucked cattle, me and Kenny. We bought a 7- by 28-foot aluminum trailer and Ford five-speed diesel truck. It all started when Kenny decided to go to a bull sale. I was working at the grocery store in Lincoln when Kenny called. He said, "Do you want to go to Texas?" I took off my apron and away we went! The seat in the back of the truck folded into a double bed-curtain with captain seats. We were trucking in style!

Bull hauling usually started in Denver, Colorado, at the livestock show in February. We hauled bulls from breeders in Montana to ranches in Texas, California, Kansas, North Carolina, and Florida; even some to Edmonton, Canada. Trucking was a good way to help our finances and pay our horse pasture bill. Down the road we went "paying the bills." We hauled just about any place we could get a load of cattle. As I remember, we got $1.50 a loaded mile. Usually came home with pretty good money. Kids kind of took care of themselves while we were away. Jackie, our oldest, took care of the younger kids when we were gone in the mountains and trucking. We relied on her for a lot when she was younger. Lots of icy roads and long hours in the truck.

Mary Faith Hoeffner (riding Profit) and Leon Meuchel (riding Badger) at the Fourth of July Parade in Lincoln, Montana, 2013.

I remember coming home from a bull haul around Christmas time. There was no time to go shopping so we gave each of the kids $5 and told them to go shopping themselves. Jerrie once said, "Mom, you have a great life, ride your horse up and down the trail all summer, and travel all over the country in winter. You eat out and stay in motels, no dishes to wash or beds to make." They thought we were on vacation!

We saw lots of country and met wonderful ranchers trucking cattle. We were always trying to make enough money for the pasture bill in the spring. Jeff helped with trucking too. We were driving along once and Jeff said to me, "Mom if you want to get home for a friend's wedding you better get behind the wheel."

Teams and Sleigh Rides

Winters are long in Lincoln, so we decided to give sleigh rides to earn a little extra Christmas money. We gave sleigh rides at the Seven Up Supper Club and at Stonewall Steak House. Our business saying went something like this...

Dashing through the Snow
With Bells on the Sleigh
Come to Lincoln and Relax
The Montana Way

We did hour-long group rides for around $100. Melvin, one of our friends, built a black and red sleigh. It was a beautiful sleigh, a ten-seater with a black frame and rolled front like the old fashion ones. Even had red wooden seats. I decided to break two of our big black horses to pull the sleigh. We started driving them to a stone boat one at a time, then put them together. Didn't take long to break them in. Two feet of snow across the meadow in winter. We made our Christmas money!

One winter one of the big horses got hit and killed on the highway. So, we used a couple pack mules, Ally and Kate, after that. We used the mules on sleigh rides, and took them in the Lincoln parade often hitched to a Conestoga wagon. You can ride, drive, or pack those mules. One time I was at the Seven Up Supper Club giving sleigh rides at Christmas time. Drove those mules home about 4 miles with the sleigh. Drove into the yard. It was dark. My dog came running out to meet us. Ally shied, gave a big lunge and broke the neck yoke. Away we went with mules partly hooked to the sleigh. I yelled to my helper to catch the head on Kate. Got them slowed down. Coulda' been a wild ride!

Snowmobiles and Tractors

Loved my sled. Kenny and I had a couple 250 Yamahas we rode to death. Many, many rides to Trixie's Bar in Ovando and Seeley Lake, Stonewall Mountain, and up to Copper Creek Bowls. Also, did a big trip to Yellowstone National Park with friends. I remember it well because I had my leg in a brace during the trip. Takes a while for broken bones to heal! I broke my leg in September riding up Scotty Creek in the Scapegoat Wilderness. I also loved my tractor. I had a 1950 Ferguson. I harrowed the meadow with it every spring, put up bailed hay! Yes, I did that too. What a life!

Mary Faith and son Jeff with mules Kate and Alley, ca. 1990s.

Baling Wire

We had a wire baler and it seemed there was that darn wire everywhere. So, I spent several days picking up wire and tossing it into our big truck. About the time I was ready to haul the wire to the dump, Ruth Glaze drove up. I said, "Ruth, get in the truck with me and we can visit on the way to the dump!" We drove to the dump and kicked the wire out of the truck bed and headed home down highway 200, talking all the way. Ruth got in her car to go home, but returned in a few minutes. I asked, "What's the problem?" She said, "Get in the car I want to show you something." Well, we drove out to the gate and here was this huge gob of wire stuck in the cattle guard. I said, "Who in the world brought all that wire back?" About that time Kenny came home from work and said, "What's going on here?" I said, "Well, you're not going to believe this, but a couple of strands of wire must have caught on the back of the truck and we drug it all the way back down Highway 200 from the dump!" He said a few choice words and "You're right, that's a little hard to believe." Anyway, it took the three men awhile to load it back on the truck. Now, isn't that a cute story?

Colts – Always Something New with Horses

We bought a good black and gray colt from the Hayford Ranch in Conrad, Montana, and later decided to acquire the mare as well. Her name was B.J. and she was half percheron and half quarter horse, our type of mountain horse. She raised a nice quarter filly; quarter percheron, and three quarter horse. We bred the two mares to a paint stud from Helena named Fox Trotter. What beautiful spotted colts we raised. Two stud colts and two fillies. They sold well.

I once had a chance to acquire a sorrel quarter horse stud named San Doc San. We raised beautiful colts from him. What fun colts! They were so cute and playful. Then came the job of halter breaking and training. We got them trained and sold! Of course, I always had my two big sorrel mountain horses, Macho and Rooster. Lots of wonderful miles on the ranch and in the mountains with those two. Wouldn't take a million dollars for either of them.

Jerrie and a Mama Grizzly Bear

Our second daughter, Jerrie, graduated from high school in Lincoln. So, during the summer she got a job as a wilderness guard for the Forest Service. Jerrie and her sister, Jackie, used to ride bareback on horses at nine years old, riding by themselves for hours in The Purple Sage Drill Team in Lincoln, so they both knew how to ride.

She stayed at Webb Lake Ranger Station and rode trails and checked on camps. No people in camps, no horses on trails, and campfires out cold! One morning she rode in to our hunting camp while we were in the backcountry and said, "Mom, I had a bear in camp last night." "Well, what happened?" I asked. She said she was in bed, lantern turned out, and heard a noise on the porch. She reached for a match to light the lantern and something took off. She looked out the window and saw a big bear running off the porch through the gate with two small cubs behind her. The next morning Jerrie rode to our camp (6 miles away) and saw many big bear tracks on the trail. She did go back to her job, but always stayed in the cabin and slept in the attic!

Mary Faith Hoeffner riding one of her colts at the Lincoln Ranch.

4 OUTFITTING

In the evenings, after all the songs are sung and stories told, we look up at the stars in the sky. It's an awesome sight. The Big Dipper, Little Dipper, and North Star, various stars lighting up the sky. Then we head for our sleeping bags and a good night's sleep. Another wonderful day in the wilderness, peaceful and quiet. – Mary Faith Hoeffner

K Lazy Three Outfitters and Guides

It all started with my dad acquiring an outfitting permit with the Forest Service for a hunting camp on Crow Creek in the mountains near Lincoln, Montana. My husband Kenny later went to work with dad guiding hunters. We all loved camping, so when dad decided to sell the outfitting business, we bought it. We got a permit, some tack, an old gray truck with a dump box, and about six horses. We were in business! Harold Barber, who was also a guide, was in the area at the time and went in as a partner with us. That didn't last long. We all had our own ideas and by that time me and Kenny had a family of five and bills to pay.

My dad's brand was K Lazy Three, so we became K Lazy Three Outfitters and Guides. Early on we worked with the Forest Service to acquire another camp we called Camp Creek. Camp Creek was true wilderness. It was and still is a very remote camp, but we loved it. There was no trail or camp in Camp Creek, so that first year we busied ourselves building a trail with help from neighbors and guides. We began with a small crew consisting of me, Kenny, and the kids. The Glaze family went up to camp with us several times and helped build a trail 2 to 3 miles up the creek. The trail crossed the creek, back and forth. Dave Harrington and Les Nader, who later became guides for us, helped build corrals and tent frames. No chain saws in the wilderness. Everything was done by hand. Grover Botkin, a gun collector and friend, helped also.

We gradually added to our six horses. I believe the first fall we had five or six hunters. Not much income for a family of seven. We worked at new brochures and finally began building up a cliental. My girls worked as waitresses at Lambkin's Café in Lincoln to earn money for school clothes and other stuff. One morning a couple guys came in for breakfast. They were hunters looking for a place to hunt. Jackie said, "My dad's an outfitter. Would you like to hunt in the backcountry?" Before you knew it, they were on the trail with Jerrie headed for our camp. They were from New York and hunted with us for many years. They would always say it's a sad day when leaving camp.

Kenny and Mary Faith Hoeffner on top of Scapegoat Mountain, ca. 1960s.

We later acquired Meadow Creek camp from Oral Zumwalt of Lincoln, Montana. Meadow Creek camp was on the East Fork of Meadow Creek. The fishing was great during the summer and camp was only about 1.5 miles from Meadow Lake. Our other camp, Camp Creek, was always a great hunting camp with big elk around. That first season we packed the blue wood cook stove in on a big brown horse. He barely made it to camp. About 250 pounds to a side. You just can't take those cook stoves apart very much. It was wonderful to cook on and we used it many years.

It had a warming oven on top and side water holder made of blue enamel. I cooked lots of turkey, steak, pancakes and eggs on it. Loved my stove, but it took lots of small sticks of wood to cook a turkey.

As the business grew we hired guides. Over the years we had many wonderful guides. Kenny and I really enjoyed our guides. They all worked hard for us. All loved the horses and hunting.

Mary Faith and Kenny Hoeffner, White River Pass, Bob Marshall Wilderness, ca. 1980s.

Skip and Holly Halmes, guides for the K Lazy Three Ranch.

Some of Our Guides (In Alphabetical Order)

Aaron Daniels—Guide and packer, great hunter and friend.

Bill Cyr—Worked both in the summer and fall as a packer and guide. Helped whenever I needed it.

Bobby Cyr—Guide, packer, always fun to be around in camp.

Bob Orr—Guide, packer, and family friend.

Brent Andersen—Was a local Lincoln guy. I remember he rode up to camp to take supplies (7 miles) and on the way home his saddle horse bucked him off…twice (that horse could buck)! So, Brent said enough of this, and he saddled up a packhorse to ride and led his saddle horse. Brent also rode out to Lincoln the time I got bucked off and had fifteen stitches put on my forehead. I went to the hospital, but was back and shot my goat. That's another story!

Dan Quie—Worked on the trail crew for the Forest Service. His dad was Al Quie, governor of Minnesota. Dan was a cowboy and came west seeking adventure. He decided he wanted to guide so he started out working with us. One time he came into camp with a pack string in the snow and cold. We were almost out of wood. Dan started cutting dead trees so we had wood and a warm camp. Dan married our youngest daughter, Penny Jo. A year later they worked with us. Penny Jo, Dan, and their beautiful baby daughter, Brooke, helped with the business. Brooke was only about six months old. Dan carried her on his horse in the saddle in front of him. I think she slept most of the way. We bathed her in a dishpan and kept her warm and fed. She survived the hunt! Penny Jo carried her 13 miles in about four hours.

Danny Lamb—Hunted with us first, and then came to guide with us. From Missouri.

Dave Harrington—Is a story by himself. He came to our ranch when he was about twelve or thirteen years old. Always said I should have raised him better, as he was like one of the family. Dave stuck around Lincoln and helped with haying, etc. Rough, tough, and liked to fight. He did well in high school rodeo, but kinda' got out of hand. He worked for LF Ranch in Augusta, but always ended up back at our place. He was one heck of a guide and packer! Married three times. Roped grizzly bears up on a ranch in Browning. He loved a big black hat, fancy boots, good horses, and saddles. And he could ride! He always sent a Christmas card, a cowboy card, and note. Or he would call. He would call and say, "I roped another one." "Another what?" I would say. "Another griz." He called me three times about roping bears. Some folks didn't believe it, but if you knew Dave you would believe it. He would do it, I knew him. Dave is gone now; passed away in 2013. Miss him. He was "one of a kind."

Dave Morgan—A great packer and guide. Dave loved to tease. One morning I went to the corral to ride out. There stood my horse with saddle on backwards and Dave standing there laughing.

Donny Hilger—Guide and packer, always fun to be around. Many good times with Donny.

Guides Dave Harrington and Les Nader, ca. 1970s.

Ed Johnson—Guide who spent many nights in camp between hunts taking care of camp, keeping the grizzly bears out!

Kenny Palmer—Guide who also helped on summer trips. Enjoyed a little whiskey with Kenny.

Kevin Cole—Was from Missouri. He came out hunting one year. Then the next year he came back and worked with us guiding and helping around the ranch. He married his girlfriend, Sue, and brought her and their two-year-old daughter, Becky, to camp. We bathed her in the dishpan. It took Sue almost one mule to pack in her Pampers diapers! Later Kevin Jr. came on trips with us.

Kevin Gardner—Was a great guy and entertainer. His poem about "Buford the Mule" was a classic. Also, a wonderful singer, story teller, and packer. Good friend and cook.

Larry Menard—Guide and packer. His family, wife Linda, and children Tell, Tawny, Katie, and Clint helped me later on the ranch with whatever needed to be done. Whether breaking colts, shoeing, or really anything, he was there to help. Thank you!

Leon Meuchel—Was part of our family. He didn't have much family, so he joined ours. What a character! Always smiling and planning something! Had a wonderful memory. He loved to recite the poems "Cremation of Sam McGee" and "Elk Hunters Creed." He knew the name of every horse we ever had. He was an entertainer and hard worker, and he loved our family. Leon loved driving teams and was good with stock. Helped me halter break the colts. We tied two on each side of a trailer and went out across the meadows. Leon is still family and shows up for Christmas and Thanksgiving. Wonderful dog trainer and "All Around Cowboy!"

Les Nader—Worked for us when we first started out. Five bucks a day, sometimes not even that. He loved the life: hunting, mountains, and horses. He became an excellent guide, but don't talk to him 'til after breakfast. He was grouchy. I remember he had a big yellow horse. It used to get "lead rope" under his tail. Horse would be bucking and Les would be cussing!

Larry Bjork—One of a kind. Loved the mountains and hunting, he would ride across any mountain no matter how steep. He laughed a lot and would give you the shirt off his back (if he had one). He could almost live in the mountains. I remember one time me and Larry Bjork were going up to Camp Creek. He had two mules with packsaddles. We were visiting like we always did. I turned around and both pack saddles were under the mule's bellies.

Lenny Orr—Also known as the "Hunter," was a hard worker. He found me on top of Scotty Creek with a broken leg. Rode 14 miles for help and a helicopter. Thank you, Lenny!

Melvin Barber—Had long hair and looked kinda like a hippie, but always had a big smile. He was a great hunter and rider. He would ride anywhere for an elk, up the mountain no matter how steep. I know because I was with him and got scared a couple of times.

Mick Tinsley—Worked with us also. I remember a horse ran away with him down the mountain through the trees and back to camp. I remember I gave him heck. "Don't you be running that horse down the trail, he's all sweated up."

Mark Young—Was one of my favorites. During one hunt with a group from Texas, Mark came into camp and said, "Come on everybody, there's a big herd of elk up Mineral Creek Basin." So me and Jeff (Jeff was a teenager then) and the Texans all rode up Bugle Mountain, a steep switchback trail, and on down the mountain about 2 miles to look across the canyon to see the elk move into the timber. Mark took Jeff and a couple hunters where they walked down to Mineral Creek Basin. It was about 5:30 am, cold, and a foot of snow. It was October 1ˢᵗ. But that's hunting. Those guys would ride or walk anywhere to get an elk.

Pat Orr—Helped us up in Camp Creek. Pat's a good shot. We had a wonderful time and guided six hunters.

Rod Krier—Great guide and packer. Excellent hunter! Always fun to be around.

Gordy Becker—Guide and packer, great help!

Skip Halmes—Guide and packer and best friends. His wife Holly also went on summer trips with us. Wonderful friends!

Ward Kemmer—Guided many years at the K Lazy Three Outfitters, many hunting and fishing trips. Great guide, packer, always made sure the work was done and the horses were fed right. Great friend!

Guide Ward Kemmer (left) with a client, ca. 1990s.

K Lazy Three Ranch, guides and hunters, ca. 1990s.

Jeff Hoeffner with a Royal Bull, ca. 1970s.

Camp

Our camp generally consisted of a large 16-by-24 foot tent with doors and flaps on each end and a dirt floor, which I swept clean of dust with a large branch. I poured dish rinse water on the floor and it became hard by fall. We had a large table covered with my red Naugahyde tablecloth. Sometimes I'd put wildflowers in tin cans on the table. We used a large wood barrel stove with a flattop for cooking. One luxury we did have was a 30-inch propane stove to bake and cook on. Cupboards we made of plywood and were set up for dishes and silverware. Two plywood cupboards were for bread and groceries. Work table along the wall with shelves beneath. An ol' cupboard behind the stove with the cast iron grill, skillets, pans, and dishpans. We also had a table for a washstand. And, we usually put up a fly outside for extra rain cover. Outside, we had lots of stumps with backs to be used as extra chairs.

I always slept in the northwest corner of the cook tent on a cot with my dog Tango underneath. We put up a tarp between my bedroom and the kitchen table. I was lucky; usually Kenny, Jeff, or one of the guides lit the big barrel stove and put on coffee on cold mornings. It was nice and warm in the cook tent. I lived in my sleeping bag from May 'til November.

We also had four 12-by-16 foot guest tents with heating stoves and clothes racks. Near camp we set up one wrangler tent and a tack tent. The guides built corrals for livestock at Meadow Creek and Camp Creek for water. Pack it in and throw it out. Lots of water buckets! We also put water buckets and washbasins in the guest tents. For the floors, either dirt or plastic, or lots of tarps. Always a big campfire pit to gather around at night for songs and stories. We packed in two big coolers with meat and fresh vegetables and set them outside the back door. It took lots of groceries for six to eight days for a group of eight fishermen or hunters. And if you forgot something, it's a long way to the grocery store or café!

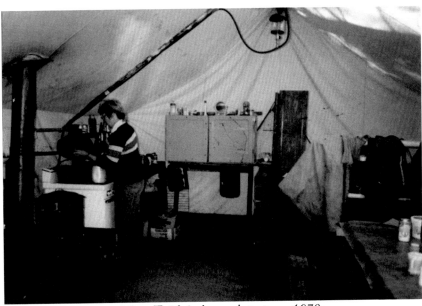

Mary Faith in her cook tent, ca. 1970s.

We fed our guests the usual menu of spaghetti or lasagna, pork chops and potatoes, onions, sauerkraut, and mushroom soup, and sometimes cowboy scalloped potatoes. We had a roasted turkey every hunt, as well as roast beef or pork. Juicy rib steak on every hunt on the last night. For lunch, sometimes hamburgers, soups, crisp lettuce salad with tomatoes. Carrot cake, chocolate pie for dessert, and sometimes hot rolls, biscuits or corn bread for a snack. Breakfast consisted of pancakes with bacon and eggs or ham, French toast, and sausage, or biscuits and gravy. No freeze-dried food in our camp! We fed them well!

Grover Botkins, Mary Faith, and Kenny Hoeffner (from left to right), 1967.

A Typical Day in Camp

Kenny up at 5:30 am to start the wood stove and put the coffee pot on. Always need a couple cups of coffee to start the day. Then wake up the guides and turn horses out to graze. A couple times I could hear horse bells clanging as they ran past the cook tent. I always waited for a warm tent and coffee, then I would crawl out of the sleeping bag. I guess I was a little spoiled. I always slept in the cook tent in one corner with a manti tarp hung between the sleeping area and kitchen. Wash up, comb hair, and put skillet and griddle on stove and start breakfast. Better start more coffee! Hot cakes and eggs, bacon, or French toast, ham, hash browns or biscuits, sausage and gravy. Big pitcher full of Tang, our favorite breakfast juice. Call guests for breakfast. They usually were gathered in the warm cook tent or had started a bonfire in the fire pit. Mornings are cool and cold. Then back to the sleeping tents to get ready for the day! We put out lunch fixings. Sometimes roast beef, or turkey left over from dinner, or lunch meat and fruit and apples or oranges and camp cookies. Probably some soda or water.

Where are we riding today? Maybe up Bugle Mountain. A good trail; steep, but the panoramic view from the top is magnificent. Look down into Meadow Creek, Meadow Lake, or to the east Olsen Peak, Red Mountain, Parker Lake. How about lunch and a little break? Better start down. Back to camp for cleanup and maybe a nap. Hopefully the cook has supper ready. Wait, I'm the cook! Last night is always steak and potatoes, salad and vegetables. How about some carrot cake or chocolate mayonnaise cake? Supper over, get out big dishpans and get with it. Wish I had a maid or a penny for every dish I've washed. My good friend Charlie Horsky always stands handy with his dish towel to wipe dishes. Heat up two big dishpans of water. A clean camp is a must! Oh, I forgot, somebody (usually me) has to pack water from the creek to keep the big kettle of water on the wood stove warm, hot, for dishes and various cleanup. Dishes clean. Hey, let's have a bonfire. Charlie will have firewood ready. By now it's time to hit the sack. See you in the morning. Good day!

Mary Faith preparing a meal at Camp Creek with Jeff and Judy, ca. 1970s.

Trip to Scapegoat with Charlie

Speaking of Charlie Horsky, he was so proud of Montana that each summer, he'd gather up his nephew, Tony Wertz, and all his lawyer friends and bring them to Montana on a pack trip. One year he decided to go to the top of Scapegoat Mountain. Me and Dan Quie and Charlie and his friends left camp on the East Fork of the Blackfoot and rode up Debreda Creek and camped for the night. Debreda Creek is at the southern base of Scapegoat. Kinda rough trail up to the top. In fact, one riderless horse lost his footing and rolled partway down the mountain. He got up and shook himself, and he walked back up to the trail.

Charlie Horsky casting on a creek in the backcountry, ca. 1990s.

Most riders walked across the hard rock trail leading to Hanging Garden and on up to the very peak of the mountain where we had lunch. All was going well until suddenly a big dark cloud rolled across the sky. The wind started blowing; guests were scrambling everywhere trying to get slickers on with thunder and lightning dancing on the peaks around us. Dan said, "We gotta get off the top of this mountain. No place to be in a thunderstorm." Horses were scared and excited. We returned to Debreda Creek Camp, everyone rain soaked! Spent the evening drying clothes near the campfire. Headed back to the East Fork Camp. Everyone said it was one fun and exciting trip!

Dan Quie, guide, pointing to something in the distance, ca. 1980s.

Jeff and Marie

One year Charlie brought his good friend, Judge Belson, and his very pretty daughter, Marie, on a trip with us. Well, one night around the campfire, I was sitting next to one of the guides. He leaned over and whispered, "Jeff is sitting pretty close to the little blonde girl." The next evening around the campfire, Marie's dad, Judge Belson, came to the campfire and said, "Where is Jeff and Marie?" Nobody knew! The next day Judge Belson and Marie had to leave camp early for the trailhead. Me and the guides took the rest of the group on a ride to Sourdough Basin. My guide said, "I bet Jeff will not be in camp when we get back." He was right. I found a note on a brown paper bag saying, "I had to go out to dinner with Marie and her dad. Promise to be back in camp early in the morning." So much for a reliable guide, Jeff! Anyway, it led to a wedding in Washington, D.C. and now a ranch at Winston, Montana, and three beautiful grandchildren: Colin, Kenny, and Caitlin. What can I say, a very romantic pack trip with a wonderful ending!

Marie Taylor Belson (later Marie Hoeffner) with Jeff Hoeffner at the Indian Meadows Trailhead, 1991.

Charlie and Tony

Charlie Horsky and Tony Wertz took pack trips with us just about everywhere. About ten years they rode with us. Charlie rode 'til he was eighty years old. His favorite thing to do around camp was to smoke his pipe! Near the end, we had to lift him on the horse, then lift him off. One particular trip Charlie brought his wife, Barbara, and his nephew, Tony Wertz. Tony really didn't like to fish. He liked to ride the trails and see new country (kinda like me). Anyway, he would say, "Mary Faith, what mountain we gonna climb this year?" I said, "Well, how about Galusha Peak?" He said, "Sounds, good." So, me and Tony and Sam Harahan saddled up and hit the trail. We rode up on Lost Pony, then on down the ridge to Galusha Peak. It's all high country. On Galusha Peak there is a rock monument, and we always added a rock to it. From the top, you are looking down into Cooney Creek. The view is from a sheer rock cliff about a thousand feet high. We had lunch and rested a little. I always hate to take the same trail back, so I asked Tony, "Why don't we drop down Devil's Staircase?"

Devil's Staircase is a rock staircase down the side of the mountain along Camp Creek Ridge. We were walking down first, leading the horses, when Sam Harahan says, "Mary Faith, I am scared of heights." I said, "Well Sam, it's a little late now! We gotta go." With a little talking and extra help, we got down the rocks and across to Camp Creek Ridge. Pretty long ridge! We rode and walked to the creek and down to the main trail back to camp. It was still 7 miles back to camp. Long day, and I still had to cook supper. The excitement of a high-country ridge makes it worth the trip, though.

On another occasion, me and Tony rode to the top of Bugle Mountain and headed down the ridge to the old mining camp. We dropped off the top down to a spring where an old tailing pile and mining shacks were located. Several old pieces of the building and diggings are still there. In fact, there was a packer up there for a while, packing out rocks in wooden pack boxes. I don't remember his name. Anyway, we had lunch at the old mine, then headed down a rough trail to the main trail at the bottom. Well, we somehow lost the main trail and ended up leading the horses down an old mining trail. Trees crisscrossed the path knee deep. Tony led the way awhile, then I took a turn finding our way leading our horses. I remembered I had on a pair of new boots and every step was agony. I just wanted to sit down and cry.

We made it back to camp and I still had to cook supper. We had about eight guests and two or three crew, around ten people. Charlie always wiped dishes for me. That was his thing. Guests helped get supper on the table, then the guides turned horses out to graze for a couple hours, usually about 1.5 hours 'til they got full. What a really great day. And always, after dark, songs around the campfire. Charlie and Barbara had wonderful voices and loved patriotic songs.

The Horsky's cabin burned down in the later years, so Tony built a beautiful five-bedroom log home and invited all his friends to visit him and his wife, Grace. Tony also built a big five-bedroom home in Puerto Vallarta, Mexico. Swimming pool! Beautiful! He invited me and Paul

Grosfield there for a ten-day visit. What a wonderful time. It was new, strange country for a country girl like me. We walked on the beach and shopped. Watched the cruise ships come into the harbor. Beautiful sunrises and sunsets across the ocean. There were chickens nearby, and every morning those roosters were a crowin'! Loved it.

Tony was killed in a head-on car crash just 4 miles out of Lincoln. His wife, Grace, was badly injured. I was crushed. He was one of my best friends I ever rode with. Always smiling and loved everyone! His door was always open.

The Chinese Wall

Each summer we led a Chinese Wall pack trip. The Chinese Wall is a high rock cliff approximately 7,600 feet high that runs along the top of the Continental Divide in the Bob Marshall Wilderness. The wall goes for approximately 12 miles. It's home to goats, griz, deer, elk, and supposedly lions. We usually went about the end of July or first of August. It's a seven to eight day trip.

When we arrive at the trailhead with our guests, we find our guides and wranglers and catch horses and mules for the trip. Horses and mules are tied along the corral for saddling. Riding saddles for horses; pack saddles for mules. After instruction for new riders and some ol' faithful riders, we give a brief introduction on how to stay on the back of that ol' pony. "A leg on each side and your mind in the middle!" Don't worry, your horse knows the way, probably better than the rider. Trust him. He'll get you down the trail.

Each rider is assigned a horse, according to the rider's ability. Kids loved Patches and Rambo. Our repeat clients, like my friend Sara Jane, liked Bo. Paul on Blaze. Bob on Johnny Walker. Lola Mae can ride anything! Florence loved a big black Tennessee Walker. New guests loved Baron, a little fox trotter, so smooth. Each guest is given a lunch for their saddle bag. Riders mount and adjust stirrups for length.

Jeff Hoeffner leading a string of mules beneath the Chinese Wall, ca. 1970s.

We might have six to ten guests, three wranglers, and cook (me), and sometimes my grandkids Jesse, Desiree, Mandy, and Shawn would come along with us. Jerrie, my daughter, went on several trips.
Boy, what would I do without her! Guests loved her, too. Kenny and Jeff packed approximately twenty head of livestock. My kitchen consisted of a wood cook stove, two sets of pack boxes we made into cupboards, two big coolers for meat, and fresh vegetables. Mules to pack teepee tents and duffle, and a big 16-by-20 foot tarp we put over our kitchen.

Several of us slept under the fly (as we called it). Kenny's wranglers saddled riding horses and sent me down the trail with guests. We each had a lunch with a sandwich, fruit, and cookie. Guests had their own water. So, we headed out while Kenny and wranglers finished packing. While we stopped for lunch, they passed us on down the trail to find a suitable campsite, generally somewhere below Indian Point. When in camp, I unpack everything. Set up our

Jeff and Kenny Hoeffner leading a pack string on a trip to the Chinese Wall, ca. 1980s.

camp, cut wood, got out Dutch ovens, dishes, and necessary pans for supper. When camp was cleaned up and dishes washed, we built a campfire and sang songs and discussed the day.

Next morning, wranglers up. Turned out horses to graze awhile. Brought them into horse pellets and tie on a high line, which is a rope strung between trees to tie horses to. Maybe a layover day, fishing, short ride to Prairie Reef Lookout. From Indian Point we head up to Grizzly Gulch overnight, then a magnificent ride along the base of the Chinese Wall in the Sun River Game Preserve. High alpine meadows with bear grass as high as a horse's shoulder and blooming in a great mass of cream colored flowers. The wall is home to many animals, but especially the mountain goat. Thirty miles south of the wall is the huge Scapegoat Mountain. Its cliff wall is high and 9,202 feet to the summit, 3 miles (on plateau).

So, we ride along. Our camp is out ahead with the pack mules and packers. We travel approximately 3 to 4 miles per hour, and it's many miles to Moose Creek where we will camp for the night. The vegetation is so fragile up next to the wall. We want to leave as little trace as possible. We look up at the massive wall and some of the guests hike up on top. It's magical, fresh, wild country. I have a picture entitled "Faces on the Wall" with a bald eagle flying high along the wall. You can almost pick out faces or half faces in the rocks.

Mary Faith riding through bear grass in the backcountry.

We set up our camp and guests pitch their tents. We put up a fly over the kitchen in case it rains. Horses let out on the hillside to graze, then brought back to camp and tied up on the highline. We build our campfire and sing and tell stories from the day. We stay at Moose Creek Camp two nights so the guests can hike and take a short ride to May Lake or Larch Hill Pass. We break camp the third day for a long, 14-mile ride down to the North Fork of the Sun River. Oh, the fishermen loved that. Best fishing ever. Men fish while ladies wade in the river or lie in the sun and relax. Two nights on the North Fork then we venture down the river to Pretty Prairie Another layover, then the ride out to Benchmark. Some call it a sad day going back to civilization, but it's a rest day for cooks and wranglers. Some of us stop in Augusta for our sad farewells and a cold beer. It was a great trip. Oh well, see you next year! We all love our Chinese Wall trips.

Pulling Camp on the North Fork of the Sun River, ca. 1980s.

Jeff Hoeffner and Jesse Morgan (Mary Faith's grandson) on a pack trip to the Chinese Wall.

The Chinese Wall, Bob Marshall Wilderness, ca. 1970s.

Thunderstorm at the Chinese Wall

I remember another time up under the wall we got caught in a big thunderstorm. We had camped at Moose Creek, close to the wall. I was ready to turn in for the night. Loved sleeping out in the open. So, Kenny and I gathered packsaddle pads to sleep on and put down a manti tarp then our sleeping bags and another tarp over us to keep off the dew. I remember a big thunderstorm came up. Oh, the lightning and thunder crackling along the cliffs. Flash! Then a big bang. Exciting! Then the rain came. I remember Kenny and I tugging on the tarp to keep the rain off. What a night. Next morning up to sunshine, so we packed up and headed out for the ride down Moose Creek to the North Fork for some excellent fishing.

Kenny Hoeffner fishing the North Fork of the Sun River, ca. 1980s.

Red Mountain

Four of our favorite fishing guys came on a pack trip with us to Red Mountain one year. In fact, now that I think about it, they came with us for about six years. Always played cribbage with Kenny and the guides. Jeff never really liked to ride up Bugle Mountain and over to Red Mountain. I would say, "Jeff, don't you want to come on the ride to Bugle Mountain?" He would say, "I never lost anything up there, mother."

Anyway, we all left the trailhead at Indian Meadows. The guides took the pack strings and I led the fishermen. On the way, we came to the Red Mountain Trailhead. I said, "You guys want to ride up Red Mountain then down into Sourdough and back to camp on the East Fork?" Sure, they wanted to go. So up Red Mountain we rode. It's steep, so we had to rest the horses from time to time. Had lunch with a wonderful panorama view of the mountain range. Red Mountain is 9,400 feet high.

After lunch we started down the mountain, down along sharp ridges with just enough room for a trail and a little riding or leading horses. Kenny was with us and always rode down. He said, "If I was meant to walk, I would have four legs." All of the sudden the horses started snorting and looking around. Kenny said, "Hold tight to the horses, there must be a bear around." We never did see the bear.

Kenny Hoeffner riding Spooks on top of Scapegoat Mountain, ca. 1970s.

There is a pretty little lake about halfway down Red Mountain. We have seen a goat there before. Anyway, headed on down the steep trail to Sourdough Basin. Seems like a long ways. I think some of the guys had sore feet when we arrived at camp. Graze horses and put them back in the corral. Fixed supper and campfire in the evening. Everybody works 'til work is done. These guys always helped with dishes. Long busy day, again. Bob, Mack, Jeff, and Jim. I will never forget them. They loved to ride and the excitement of being on top of the world.

These guys also took trips to the Chinese Wall and Big Horn Lake with us. Always a fun bunch. Once, while riding the High Trail around Caribou Peak, one of the guides decided to ride a mule. I said, "That mule hasn't been ridden this year!" But oh well, he rode him. We were traveling along a high ridge when I looked back and the mule was bucking down off the side of the mountain. "What can I do?" I thought, "We'll be picking him up at the bottom of the mountain." Luckily, the mule bucked him off, no injury (except his pride). He got back on and road him the rest of the trip.

Big Horn Lake

Another favorite of our guests was the trip to Big Horn Lake. We packed in at the trailhead at Alice Creek Basin and on up the ridge to the Continental Divide Trail, then down the ridge to Valley of the Moon where we found water and camped for two days. The next day we'd take our guests up the Divide Trail a couple of miles (more or less) over the Continental Divide, then drop down into Big Horn Lake for some excellent fishing and swimming. The lake was clear and the fish were always hungry. How deep is Big Horn Lake? I do not know, but the story goes one year the fish were starving so some wranglers shot an old horse and pushed him on a raft out on the lake to feed the fish that winter. Just a story I heard.

On one trip to Big Horn Lake we took Brett Todd, friend Audie Solvie, and Audie's sons, and granddaughter. We rode up from Alice Creek and camped at Valley of the Moon. The next day, the horses got loose and Brett went after them, so I took our red pack mule, our friend Audie, and his family, and we rode to Big Horn Lake for fishing, swimming, and lunch while Brett chased horses most of the day. He finally came back to camp about 4:00 pm with the horses. All he said was, "Where's supper?"

Another trip to Big Horn Lake that comes to mind involved a couple ladies. They wanted to ride so we took them. and my three granddaughters. Larry Bjork was the packer and Kevin Gardner was the guide. Up the Middle Fork to Black Tail Pass we went, then up the Continental Divide Trail to a small spring and meadow for horses. It was a beautiful little camp in the high country. We set up camp, had supper and a big bonfire, and went to sleep in our teepee tents. I remember one of the girls saying, "Grandma, I think I heard something moving around outside." I said, "It's just the horses or the wind." The next morning there were bear tracks that circled camp.

Granddaughters Mandy, Brooke, and Desiree, on a ride with Mary Faith.

Entertainment in the Wilderness Camp

Leon Meuchel, one of our wranglers and guides, did a super job reciting the poem "Cremation of Sam McGee!" Kenny always recited the "Elk Hunter's Creed." Our good friend Charlie Horsky's favorite songs to sing around the campfire were "God Bless America," "Star Spangled Banner," and "Montana, Glory of the West." Charlie was always patriotic. Guide Kevin Gardner was exciting to listen to. Everyone loved his poem about "Buford the Mule." Everything seemed more fun with Kevin in camp. My husband Kenny had a Phil-Harris song that was great for kids. He couldn't carry a tune, but repeated "Elmer and the Bear" every trip. It went something like this:

Now Elmer Jones arose at dawn,
and he put his huntin' britches on,
and looked up at his shotgun on the wall.
He made his mind up then and there
To bag himself a mess of bear
at huntin' he had plenty on the ball.

So he milked the cows, and slopped the hogs,
Kissed his wife, and called the dog,

Picked up his gun and lit out on his quest.
He crossed the creek and hit the trees,
Threw back his head and sniffed the breeze,
Let out a yell and pounded on his chest.

Here comes Elmer, Elmer's got his gun
Here comes Elmer, run, bear, run.

Now he hunted all the morning through,
But not a bear come into view,
While his stock sat on the kitchen range,
Ahh, he was tired as he could be
Of lamb and chicken fricassee
And he craved a mess of bear meat for a change.

Now Elmer's mind was in a fog,
So he paused and sat down on a log
To put his faculties back into groove.
He heard a noise and standing there
Before him was a grizzly bear.
He decided it was time he made his move.

He picked up his gun and spun around
But mister bear just held his ground
And he said "It is either me or thou."
The gun refused to go, and he knew someone had to go
So he said, "So long, I'm leavin' as of now!"

So Elmer's shoulders sprouted wings,
His feet developed inner springs.
To linger longer, he was disinclined.
He ran so fast through muck and mire,
His ankles set his socks on fire,
And still that bear kept comin' on behind.

A deer with antlers eight feet wide,
Got in the way of Elmer's stride,
As both of them were heading for the brush.
Elmer said, "Now listen, son,

If that's the fastest you can run,
Move over, cause I'm really in a rush!"

Well that bear was gainin' inch by inch,
And soon he reached out for the clinch.
As Elmer saw the fence around his place.
He leaped the fence and landed hard,
Jumped sixty feet across the yard
And slammed the kitchen door in bruin's face.

Now the bear was tryin' to get inside
And Elmer sought a place to hide,
Then Mrs. Jones began to pull her hair.
She said, "This fuss has gotta stop,
Why don't you just let the matter drop?"
He said, "Honey, why don't you go and tell that to the bear!"

She said, "Now listen, goon,
What makes you think you're Daniel Boone?
Whose appetite on bear meat used to thrive?"
He said, "I'm sure that you're aware
That Daniel always kills his bear.
But honey, I brung this one home alive!"

My favorite songs to sing around the fire were old favorites. "When the Works All Done this Fall," "Bad Brama Bull," "Strawberry Roan," "Little Joe the Wrangler," "Red River Valley," "You Are My Sunshine," and, of course, "Western Skies" by Chris Ledoux. While around the bonfire everyone would tell stories about the big fish that got away. Everybody had a story!

Fall Hunting Season

Leaves turning orange and yellow meant that summer fishing and packing trips were over and hunting season was coming. Hunting season meant lots of work and good friends returning to hunt elk and deer that live in our mountains. Our hunting season began with packing hay to camp. Manti up the hay and tie to side of a horse or mule! About 75 pounds to a side. It took about 300 bales more or less to get us through the season. I remember a time when Jackie and our good friend Nyleen Anderson were supposed to be coming to Camp Creek with Les Nader on a hay trip. Les was supposed to leave at noon, but the girls didn't arrive until 2:00 pm. It's a 13-mile ride to camp, and it was cold, very cold. I swear the two girls were nearly frozen when they arrived at Camp Creek.

We had two hunting camps—one at Camp Creek and another at Meadow Creek—each 7 miles apart. So that meant one cook tent, two sleeping tents, wrangler tent, and tack tent at each camp. Pots and pans and one cook (me) and two wranglers or guides depending on the number of hunters. With hunting there are many factors to consider: hunter ability and physical condition as well as weather. With the weather you just never know. Fall can be hot and dry, lots of dusty trails. Forest Service would caution us on sparks from horseshoes. Dead-out campfires or no campfires at all. Fall can be cold with icy trails. Horses can slide on the trials so you better watch out. Sometimes ice on the North Fork crossing and other streams. I remember a trip when it dipped to -30°F. We had to chop ice to get water from Meadow Creek. Orange juice froze on the kitchen table and everybody huddled around the big wood stove. I remember another hunt in late October when we had to bring three big elk heads and horns into the cook tent. Had to thaw them out to skin them. Horses sometimes stood in muddy corrals and had their bridle leather frozen to them. We had to bring in the bits and warm them so they didn't freeze to the horses' tongues. You had to keep all this in mind when guiding hunters.

Once the hunters are in camp it's up at 4:30 am. Coffee, breakfast, and saddle up the horses. Hurry and get a move on. Get those hunters out on the mountain by daylight. That means a couple miles riding in the dark. Hope the guides know the trail! Horses can see in the dark, sometimes back to camp in the dark. In camp everyone worked 'til work is done, including the guests at times. This is real hunting. The hunters spend their days up on the mountain with a spotting scope or just sit and watch for the movement of elk or deer. They are out at daylight 'til mid-morning then back in the timber. We send our guides and hunters to various favorite spots. Usually one guide and two hunters, and they usually hunt 'til dark.

Mary Faith and her prize elk taken in the backcountry, 1997.

That gives me a busy day of baking and maybe some hot soup for lunch in case anyone comes back early. We always send a brown bag lunch with the hunters. I might cook a turkey, stuffing, potatoes and veggies or salad. We had turkey on each hunt, or a big beef roast with lots of potatoes and veggies. Maybe meat loaf and corn on the cob, hot bread rolls, corn bread, or biscuits. Sometimes fry bread. Hunters like that. No dried food in this camp.

Anyway, it's a busy day. I might let the horses out to graze, but only one and a half hours then bring them in. During the day I always listen for rifle shots. Maybe someone got a big bull! It's always exciting each day as the hunters have a story to tell. Or, if we don't have a lot of hunters in camp, I might saddle my horse, take my rifle, and do a little riding and hunting myself.

On one outfitting trip, I got myself into some trouble. I had supper ready, already baked a cake and had a chicken out to roast. So, I took my new horse, Fly, up Scotty Creek hunting. It was a beautiful day, but cold. Elk tracks everywhere. I was sitting there on top of Fly thinking about who knows what when Fly grazed between two trees. There was room for him, but not me and my saddle. He brushed me off backwards and I fell. I felt my knee snap as I hit the ground. Oh boy! Here I am on top of Scotty Creek with a broken leg. It was below zero and I was lying in twelve inches of snow. I sat there trying to decide what to do. Everyone was out hunting. Kenny out packing an elk to Lincoln; no one would be home until dark. Decided I best stay there! Fly went off grazing. I found Kenny's cigarette lighter in my pocket along with my hunting license and a Kleenex. I reached for some pine needles and branches, slid over next to a big log and got a fire started. Unzipped my chaps and slid them under me. There I sat. I fell about 10:30 am. I knew the hunters were way over on Blondy Creek where Kenny had just packed an elk off. While he was packing the elk, he saw a big grizzly watching him, but luckily it didn't bother him. I hoped it wouldn't bother me either.

I sat in the snow looking at my watch. 1:00 pm. Everyone was likely on Blondy Creek eating lunch. 2:00 pm. Hunters and guides hunting. 4:00 pm. Wish someone would find me! Then, between 5:00 and 6:00 pm I heard a shot over by Sourdough. "Yep, they shot an elk," I thought. I was getting tired of keeping the fire going; could only reach so far for branches. The temperature continued to fall. It was so cold. If I sat still my leg didn't hurt, but it was getting to be a long day. Finally, I heard a voice saying "Mary Faith, what are doing up here?" Thank God, it was Lenny Orr. He said, "Come on, get on this horse behind me!" I said, "I can't, I think I broke my leg." By that time, it was about 7:00 pm. Lenny fired three shots and Jeff answered with three more. Lenny took off for camp. He sent Jeff and three hunters up Scotty Creek then headed out for the phone at the Forest Service station 13 miles away. Jeff and the hunters from Princeton, Iowa, brought coffee, sandwiches, and pills.

It was about 10:00 am the next morning when a helicopter flew over us, but didn't find me because I was up on the mountain. Jeff and the hunters built three fires to keep warm. They put green branches on for smoke for the helicopter to see. It's a long story, but they finally landed one ski on the mountain and set down long enough to toss me in the helicopter. I finally made it to Great Falls where Kenny and Judy waited at the hospital. I had a fractured knee and was out of the hunting camp for the season. Kenny had to cook and hated it!

Mercy Flight helicopter on top of Scotty Creek with Jeff Hoeffner, guides Lenny Orr and Skip Halmes, and clients.

Mary Faith recovering from a broken leg at home with her husband Kenny.

The Wood Cutter

Spending time in camp can be wonderful, however, there are some risks. I remember we had a fellow cutting wood for us one season. He decided to take a break and go hunting. He tied his horse to the tree along the trail over by Twin Lakes and started on his hunt up the mountain. It began snowing hard. By morning there was a foot of fluffy white snow on the ground, and it continued snowing. When he didn't come back to camp, we rode the ridge tops looking for him and shot up lots of ammo. He was out three days and two nights. We sent for a helicopter. He had shot up all his shells before he finally heard Kenny shoot up on Lost Pony. He walked up there and followed the horse tracks back to camp. I remember he was one tired and hungry hunter. He thought he had met his end. He went home and changed his life for the better. Came to visit every year after that!

Meat pole with frozen elk hanging in camp, ca. 1970s.

Mary Faith after a successful hunt, ca. 1970s.

The Elk Hunters Creed

It's always a big day when there's meat in camp. But better take it to the trailhead in case there's a bear around. The bears, ravens, and other scavengers get the gut pile. They clean it up in no time. You can always tell where there is a kill because ravens will be circling the area. We have a poem that tells it all about how proud a man can be if he kills the mighty stag. The hunt usually ends with a steak for supper and a bunch of happy hunters around the campfire each reciting lines from the following poem:

The Elk Hunter's Creed

This head on the wall is to prove to all that he of the mighty spread is the only game that's worth the name and so we saved his head.

For the elk still stands in this western land, as the greatest beast of all, and to seek him out or do without is the theme of the sportsmen's call.

The red man's cow has vanished now, so too has the grizzly bear, elk is the only game that's worth the name, unless you want a hare.

But the Indians' bow was far too slow to strike this great one dead, but now we can with skill of men, and bullets made of lead. He was forced to go when his food ran low, so perhaps he didn't cheat, he shot a cow as some do now and say they hunt for meat.

The elk live high in the mountain sky akin to the mountain sheep, in wind and snow of forty below when even the bear must sleep. He will bugle his call to the ears of all, 'til we meet at the pearly gate, he will wind his way 'til judgment day if given a chance to mate.

The bear, the moose the Canadian goose, are easy game when found, but come with me and you'll agree we've covered a lot of ground. Your shots may score a ten or more but on elk that won't quite do, for he'll leave that place without a trace even though his heart is shot through.

So all you boys with your popgun toys if it's a man you want to be, so get your gun and we'll have some fun when the elk calls follow me! For heed not I of wintry sky or an untracked forest hill for I will ride with any guide until I make my kill.

For I want you to know and I'm telling you so, he has a right to brag, for he is a man who has proven he can conquer the mighty stag.

Mary Faith and her elk, Lincoln, Montana, 2014.

My Elk Hunt

I got my elk fall of 1991. It was the 20th of November; hunting season about over, so me and Jeff and Melvin Barber took a string of mules up the North Fork to pull our Camp Creek camp. Rode up along the river past North Fork cabin along the switchbacks to North Fork Falls. While riding along, Melvin hollered, "There's a bull!" Sure enough, across a ravine on the hillside about 350 yards was a big six point. Snow was about one and one-half feet deep at the time and we had on heavy clothes. Jeff said, "Come on, mom, get your gun." Melvin held the mule string and Jeff and I ran down the trail to get a shot. I remember Jeff saying "Ok, mom, take a shot" So I did, but knew I missed. Jeff's gun jammed, so I took another shot and hit him. He stood there on the hillside stunned, waving those big horns around looking to see where the shots came from.

I carried a .284 and Jeff a 7mm. Jeff got his gun working and we finished the elk. Jeff wasn't sure I hit him. But in dressing him out we found the bullet from my .284. The bull was beautiful, about 14 years old. We rode on into Camp Creek, packed up the tents, cots, stove and cooking stuff. Stayed one night and rode out with my elk. Jeff let me lead the mules with the elk. I was one proud and happy hunter. We put my tag on him. Thanks, Melvin!

My Goat Hunt

I hunted more than just elk, you know. I finally got that goat license! So, it's time to get that goat. A few months earlier I'd been hunting up Bugle Mountain and had a little wreck on my horse, Blaze. Ended up on another helicopter ride to St. Pete's Hospital in Helena with a concussion and a bunch of stitches in my head. Penny Jo was in camp that fall helping cook. She's the one who saw my horse at the corrals that evening without me on it! She went and found help and got me to the hospital. Good thing for Penny Jo! I was back on my feet before too long. I went to see my doctor soon after the fall and he said, "Ok, Mary Faith, go get your goat!"

Back at Camp Creek, Judy, Penny Jo, and I were cooking. It was wonderful to have my girls in camp. They were such a big help. Kenny came by and said he had seen a goat up Lost Pony, way up on top. So, up Lost Pony Dan Quie guided me and Judy. Rode up toward Galusha Peak. Kenny spotted a goat on a cliff on top of the mountain. So, Dan, Judy, and I circled around and came in below the goat. I shot several times. The goat started moving a little so I took Dan's gun, a 30-6, and shot him. He came tumbling down towards us. Kenny yelled, "Stop him," so the goat wouldn't fall to the bottom of the mountain. Dan ran toward him and grabbed him by the horns. My goat's horn is about 7 to 8 inches, but I'd never shoot another.

I sure loved hunting, riding, and roaming around different trails. My favorites were the trails up Lost Pony and around Twin Lakes, Scotty Creek, and Scotty Creek Ridge, up Bugle Mountain, and through Sourdough Basin. But watch out for bear! One time I was riding up Sourdough Basin and saw bear hair on a tree. It was almost as high as me on my horse. A big bear. I headed down the trail and back to camp. Sometimes we looked out the door to see a big moose in the creek. Exciting never knowing what's around the corner or over the next mountain. Nothing like riding a good horse in new country.

Left to right: guide Dan Quie, Mary Faith and Kenny Hoeffner. Judy Hoeffner taking photo.

Kenny, Penny Jo, Jeff, Mary Faith, and a client on top of Lost Pony, ca. 1960s.

Hunting with Judy

All the girls helped cook during fall hunting season. I remember Judy helped one fall when we decided to go hunting up Scotty Creek above Twin Lakes. We were following big elk tracks when all of the sudden Judy said, "Mother, what are we doing on top of this mountain in about a foot of snow?" You know, I've always really loved hunting. What else can I say? I would get my supper ready (maybe bake a cake) then saddle my horse and go hunting. I knew all the hot spots: Lost Pony, Twin Lakes, Scotty Creek, and Dry Fork Trail. Rode my horse out many times and just followed elk tracks.

Wonderful Times in Camp

We had so many wonderful times in camp during hunting season it's hard to write them all down. The hunters we met came from all walks of life, but shooting a big bull elk or buck was their ultimate dream! They rode to the top of the mountain in the dark before daylight and rode back to camp in the dark in all types of weather.

Mary Faith and daughter Judy cooking in camp.

and loved it. I remember the group of Texans always hunted the second week of October and always shot elk. One year Mr. Kimbro, Mr. Lacky, Mr. Shell, and Bobby Whittingham from Texas killed theirs up Bugle Mountain in about two feet of snow. Two five points. I remember Kenny had a heck of a time packing them off the mountain!

We had a grizzly in camp now and then. One time a bear tore down the outhouse and took the toilet seat. Guys came to the kitchen and said, "Mary Faith, have you been to the outhouse, because there isn't one!" That bear came into camp and tore the outside of a tent then took off with the toilet seat around its head. We had one large 500-pound griz that kept trying to get the meat off the meat pole. We would turn out the lantern in the tent and sure enough he would be trying to take an elk quarter. One night Kenny said, "I am tired of that damn bear." I held the tent flap open and he shot him. The hunters got up when they heard the shot. Les Nader said, "You should wear more clothes, Mary Faith." I was holding the lantern in my PJs. Found the bear the next day along the horse trail, dead. It took three horses to drag the carcass away from the trail. A horse would not go down the trail with the smell of bear around.

Mary Faith and Kenny Hoeffner with a Montana grizzly killed September 20, 1973.

I never really worried about bears much. We kinda left them alone and they left us alone. For example, I remember one evening when we first started our outfitting business, me and Kenny went up Camp Creek to bring the camp out. We stayed all night and the next day started packing up tents, cots, pots, and pans. While we were working, we noticed the horses all looking at the east side of the corral. Sure enough we saw a bear walking along the corral. We watched over our shoulders, but kept packing (lots to pack). I looked up and the bear (about a two year old) was walking down the trail toward us. I said "Kenny you better do something." He had a 30-30 and shot in front of him a couple times. The young griz jumped and ran up the mountain, but not far. We packed up the horses and headed out down the trail to camp at Indian Meadows. Sure glad we didn't stay in Camp Creek that night. We left about 4:00 pm and it was pitch black when we finally passed Webb Lake and rode on into Indian Meadows. Camp Creek was 17 miles from the trailhead.

Speaking of bears, on one trip into the backcountry a group of California fishermen (Jim, Mac, Jeff, and Bob) wanted to see a bear, so we packed a lunch and rode up Scotty Creek. While heading up on the trail, we saw a big bear. They said, "What do we do?" I answered, "Keep going, he will leave." We rode on up the ridge and watched the bear across Scotty Creek. Later we saw a blonde-colored bear. Made their day! Watched those two bears all day.

We kinda had a little community up there in the backcountry. People would sometimes stop in to say hello, even though we were 14 miles from the nearest trailhead. My cousins Ron and Ray Mills stopped in for cookies. Forest Service crews stopped by for baked cookies and hot bread and sometimes for supper. Dave Harrington who lived up Arrasta Creek stopped by often and Cody Spence who was always traveling around stopped in. They were always welcome. We made good friends and played plenty of poker.

I remember Kenny left me to guide six to eight hunters in to camp one time. During the ride into camp, some of them accidentally turned off the main line trail. When Kenny arrived, he asked where the rest of the hunters were (I had four with me). "They missed the trail into Camp Creek," I said. Kenny rode down the trail to bring them back. Kenny said "Oh well, they will be back when they get hungry."

Last Week in Camp Creek

Sometimes the work was tough. By the end of the season I was tired. I remember the last week in Camp Creek one season. It was November, cold, snowy, with icy trails. I opened my eyes and saw my breath in the tent. Jeff stood over me. "It's 4:00 am; let's go, mom, hunters to feed." I said, "I just don't want to do this no more." Jeff said, "Just three more days, mom. You can do it, just three more days."

Camp at Meadow Creek in late November, ca. 1980s.

Jeff Hoeffner and guide Ward Kemmer leading a pack string out of Meadow Creek Camp in late fall.

Happy Times – Surprise Party

We had just packed out of the mountains; a fishing trip. Our kids picked us up at the trailhead at Indian Meadows. They drove through town for something or other. I remember thinking, "What's going on at the park?" A bunch of people had gathered there. Come to find out, friends and family planned our 25th wedding anniversary party. What a wonderful surprise. Big cake and ice cream! Another great day. A great party.

Mary Faith and Kenny Hoeffner at their surprise 25th wedding anniversary party in Lincoln, Montana, 1977.

Wildflowers

Craighead and Craighead say there are about 590 species of plants in the Rocky Mountain Region. The bitterroot, the state flower of Montana, is one of my favorites. White to pink, with white flowers. Bitterroot is one of the early flowers, appears as soon as snow melts. The Indians used this root for food. The Bitterroot Valley was named after it. The sulphur flower is also interesting. My favorite, though, is the glacier lily. Comes up right behind the snowmelt. Larkspur, shootingstar, steershead, pine drops, grass of parnassus, Indian paintbrush, alpine forget-me-not, red monk flower, mountain penstemon, buttercup. I love them all.

We once took a group of John Craighead's students on a trip to Scapegoat Mountain. John Criaghcad and his brother Frank were pioneers in grizzly bear research. It was a privilege to help them in their work. They hiked and we packed their duffels and had one extra riding horse. The horse had a rider most of the trip! Craighead was doing a grizzly bear study at the head of Canyon Creek under Scapegoat Mountain. We rode to top of Scapegoat and all over that mountain, me and Kenny as guides!

Mary Faith and Kenny Hoeffner guiding a group of John and Frank Craighead's students in the Scapegoat Wilderness, ca. 1970s.

Horse Bells

When in the backcountry we ran the horses out of the corral at night and gathered them up in the morning. Put horse bells on the leaders (a strap with a bell round their neck, maybe five or six bells). Oh, I loved the sound of horse bells. Horses coming into camp was music to my ears. When you heard the bells, you knew you would not be on foot for the day! We sometimes grazed the horses up Lost Pony for the night at the East Fork Camp or up the snow slides from Meadow Creek. I loved herding horses. If they took a notion and got ahead of you on the trail it would mean a wild ride to the trailhead and back. I remember one horse named Ragweed. He would head out to the trailhead every chance he got. Twenty below zero one day and that horse got away. Wild ride! Cold ride! Melvin herded them back. Dave would bring horses down from Camp Creek, bells ringing, Dave cussing!

Mary Faith riding Badger in the backcountry.

Tough Times – When the Horses Died

The winter of 1975 we brought the horses home from winter pasture and turned them out to pasture next to the ranch on the Big Blackfoot River. We had a big snowstorm and thought the horses would come home. After a couple of days, we went to look for them. Kenny and Judy found thirteen head dead in the river. Sad, sad day for the family. Some of the girls' favorite horses died.

Our horses died the same time that the Mike Horse Mine tailing ponds washed out. All the toxins washed down the river where the horses were drinking. We had the state vet check them and he said they died of cyanide poisoning. Their throats were burned. Our friends in Lincoln and relatives and hunters from Texas put on a dinner and dance to help us raise money to buy horses. We went to the horse sales to replace the horses. However, those horses could never be replaced.

Poster from the Hoeffner's Benefit Dance, 1976.

Tough Times – My Dad, L. Kenneth McLean

Back in 1965 my dad bought a small lodge named Evergreen Cabins on Rodger's Pass. After selling the outfitting business to me and Kenny, he kept a few horses at the cabins and took people riding and hunting. In fact, Buck, one of our horses, was there. It was Labor Day weekend 1977 when two men, Andrew Sunday and Jim Wilson, and Wilson's girlfriend Donna Mitchell and her three-year-old daughter named Shirley, parked their car across the road from Evergreen Cabins. They were from Lincoln, Nebraska, and we later learned they had been travelling around the country stealing. Sunday and Wilson broke into the tack room and stole horses and rifles from dad's cabin with the idea of going into the backcountry to live off the land. They took the horses up the Continental Divide trail, over the pass into Alice Creek.

L. Kenneth McLean in the Scapegoat Wilderness, ca. 1970s.

Two days later my dad and stepmother Marion came to the cabins and saw the horses were missing. They called a few neighbors and the game warden, Larry Davis, and started searching for them. Dad came to our place in Lincoln, but we were in camp getting ready for hunting season. He and Marion drove up Alice Creek and spotted Sunday, Wilson, and Mitchell in a grassy meadow. Dad drove a blue

International pickup back then. When they saw the horses, they drove over toward them. He had his rifle, and my stepmother Marion was with him. She had her revolver. My dad confronted the men saying, "What the hell are you doing with my horses?" Andrew Sunday drew his rifle and shot my dad in the leg then knocked him to the ground. Marion and my dad fired back, but missed. Sunday pointed the barrel at the back of dad's head and pulled the trigger. In the excitement, Wilson swung his gun around and shot Marion in the face killing her instantly.

I remember me and Kenny and guide Dan Quie were all in camp. We were setting up for hunting season. Hunting season started the 15th of September. We were getting the hay and groceries and everything ready when two Forest Service guys arrived. They said, "Kenny, you better come down here, we have something to talk to you about." So, Kenny went down to the corral to talk to them. After a while he came back up to the tent and said, "Mary Faith, you better sit down." I said, "What's the matter?" He said, "Well, your dad's been shot and killed." I said, "Oh poor Marion." The men kinda   looked at each other and they said, "Well, she's gone too."

We rode out. It was the longest ride I ever rode, those 13 miles. It turns out a sheep herder found dad and Marion's bodies in the meadow near Alice Creek where the killers left them. The sheepherder said dad's shirt was blowing in the wind above green grass. We later learned that the killers went into Lincoln and played pool at Lambkin's Bar for a while before stealing a different car and driving to Missoula. They were arrested a few days later in Pendleton, Oregon, at a Western Union Telegram office. They were brought back to Montana and tried for murder. Wilson agreed to testify against Sunday. He described what happened in court:

Wilson: I seen the first shot. I seen Mr. McLean fall.

Court: Where did it go?

Wilson: Hit Mr. McLean in the leg.

Court: Then what happened?

Wilson: Mr. McLean fell, and I turned my horse and ran.

Court: Did you hear him say anything?

Wilson: I heard Mr. McLean say, "You son of a bitch."

Court: And you turned you horse?

Wilson: And I ran. Had the baby on there with me.

Court: Where did you go?

Wilson: About, maybe, 50 or 60 feet from where it started.

Court: Where was Donna at this time?

Wilson: Donna was on the ground. At the time I stopped the horse, I didn't know where she was until I stopped the horse.

Court: How far did you go with the horse?

Wilson: Maybe 50 or 60 feet from where it started.

Court: What did you do there?

Wilson: I took the baby by the arm and leaned over the saddle and laid her on the ground.

Court: Then what did you do?

Wilson: I got off the horse.

Court: How did you get off the horse?

Wilson: Swung my leg over the front of the horse. Couldn't get off any other way.

Court: Did you have a weapon in your hands?

Wilson: At that time, no, sir.

Court: You said you started to yell at Donna – what did you say?

Wilson: I told Donna to get the hell over here and get the baby and get out of here.

Court: Then what?

Wilson: I got off the horse, and I was trying to untie the gun off the saddle. I had it tied on the side.

Court: Did you hear anything in the time period that you turned your horse and dropped the baby off?

Wilson: Shooting.

Court: How much shooting?

Wilson: Quite a bit

Court: Do you have any idea the number of shots?

Wilson: Ten or fifteen shots at least.

Court: Okay.

Wilson: Hard to judge.

Court: And as you were untying the gun – what gun did you have?

Wilson: A 22.250

Court: Did you get it untied?

Wilson: No, sir, I jerked it loose.

Court: Then what did you do?

Wilson: I turned and started back towards where the McLeans were.

Court: Where was Sunday at this time?

Wilson: He was walking towards Mr. McLean. Mr. McLean was on the ground.

Court: Did the defendant fire any shots after you had your gun in your hands?

Wilson: No, he didn't.

Court: What did you do as you were approaching?

Wilson: I was walking by, and I didn't know where Mrs. McLean was, and as I went by I seen a movement and I just turned and fired.

Court: Do you know what happened with the bullet?

Wilson: Yes, it hit Mrs. McLean in the face.

Both Wilson and Sunday were tried and convicted for the murders. Wilson was sentenced to 100 years and Sunday 240 years. Both were sent to the prison in Deer Lodge. Donna Mitchell was sentenced to 8 years at the Life Skills Center for Women in Billings where she got to see her daughter on weekends. She served a little over a year before the state granted her parole. Nobody could believe she got off so easy. Friends gathered petitions with over 450 signatures telling the parole board to reconsider, but the letters showed up late and she was let off. People even wrote to Governor Thomas Judge, but nothing happened.

During the trial it came out that Andrew Sunday was the real mastermind and Jim Wilson, Donna Mitchell, and the three year old were more or less in the wrong place at the wrong time. James Wilson wrote the family a letter apologizing for what he did:

To the family of Mr. and Mrs. McLean:

I have wanted to write this letter ever since I was brought back to Helena. I have put it off for two reasons, one was Sunday's trial, and the other was that I just didn't have the courage. Please understand that I'm not looking for understanding or forgiveness. My part in what happened was wrong. I admit that. I know saying that I'm sorry doesn't change anything, but please believe me. I am sorry. If there was anything that I could do to change what has happened, I would gladly do so. I'm sure that there are some questions that members of the family would like answered. If there is anything I can do to answer any of those questions please contact Mr. Charles Gravely. I will do everything in my power to help you get the answers to your questions.

Thank you for taking the time to read this.
Jim Wilson

7-29-78

To the family of Mr. & Mrs. McLean:

I have wanted to write this letter ever since I was brought back to Helena. I have put it off for two reasons, one was Sundays trial, and the other was that I just didn't have the courage.

Please understand that I'm not looking for understanding or forgiveness. My part in what happened was wrong, I admit that. I know saying that I'm sorry doesn't change anything, but please believe me, I am sorry. If there was anything that I could do to change what has happened, I would gladly do so.

I'm sure that there are some questions that members of the family would like answered, If there is anything I can do to answer any of those questions, Please contact Mr. Charles Hamby. I will do everything in my power to help you get the answers to your questions.

Thank you for taking the time to read this

Jim Wilson

Letter from James Wilson to the families of L. Kenneth and Marion McLean, 1978.

The state had a parole board meeting for Jim Wilson a few years ago. He'd been in for about 25 years. I was feeling lenient about things, then I read the pathologist report about the way he and Sunday killed my dad and stepmother. After reading how they executed them I said, "No way are they going to get out." You know, it was just by chance that they stopped right there. It was just by chance they decided to take horses over the mountains. Those were tough times! We had a nice memorial for dad and Marion. I saved the tributes written to them both.

In Memory of L. Kenneth McLean

The man was quiet and shy, but he walked tall.
And you could count on him at your beck and call.
He was always well dressed, in his western attire.
And was indeed a man anyone could admire.

He was very well liked, this man of renown.
Especially by folks, in that "Lincoln" town.
His neighbors will remember how helpful he's been.
That tall, lean man they all called "Ken."

He'll be remembered well, this soft spoken man.
"Cause he'd been quite a rancher, since his time began.
But he led a nice simple life you see.
And was just "plain folks," like you or me.
He had three devoted daughters, he loved so.
And two fine sons, that he watched grow.
I'm sure they wander fondly down memory lane.
When they think of their "Dad"
      L. Kenneth McLean.

He'll be remembered for his boots and Stetson hat.
If he's ever said hello, or stopped to chat.
His ready smile, and his easy way.
Maybe gave a silver lining to somebody's day.
He was friendly to people, if he knew them or not.
From the older folks, to the tiniest tot.
Why his friends remember him, we need not explain.
They all knew him well,
      L. Kenneth McLean.

Besides farming and ranching, other jobs he knew.
He once delivered the mail, maybe to me or you.
One more place he worked where he was inspired.
That was for "Cascade County" and from there he retired.
And because of that, he was known far and wide.
He loved that place, every hill and glen.
The man who walked tall, the man called "Ken."

He stood up for his rights as well he should.
He protected what was his, as anyone would.
He tried to rely on the old western ways.
If it was yours, it was yours, and nothing more to say.
But fate played a trick, that wasn't quite fair.
He went looking for what was his, and met his maker out there.

If he'd have been a coward, like a lot of other men
He would still be here, the man called "Ken."

It was a Labor Day weekend, all this took place.
The weather was fine, it had been for days.
There was a few people there, to do what they could.
To help him with his supply of winter firewood.
That night someone stole his horses and tack.
And he went out to find them, and bring them back.
He found what was his, but nothing did he gain.
He died fighting for what was his
  L. Kenneth McLean

I've heard people say, they've lost someone dear.
That doesn't mean they're lost, just because they're not here.
Their memory will live, I know this is true.
If you loved them and they loved you.
All the good things they've done while they were here.
Will always keep them close and dear.
God helps keep our love, and faith and then.
You'll know he's not lost, not this man, not "Ken."

Time heals all wounds, Yes this is so.
It's been happening since time began, you know.
Just remember all the things he loved to do.
Riding, roping, watching a sunset too.
And he'd want you, his loved ones to be glad.
And be happy, for the good life that he had.
Because of his love you should never complain.
He was your "Dad" and he loved you.
  L. Kenneth McLean

    By Pearl Alfson
    sister to L. Kenneth McLean's
    deceased wife Marion Lone McLean

In Memoriam

Our Little Sister
In the tiny pink bundle, so cuddly and sweet,
With two tiny hands, and two tiny feet
A cute turned up nose, and blond curly hair,
We say a blue-eyed angel, with skin so fair.
Nine brothers and sisters looked down in awe
At the beautiful little miracle that we saw.
Mom looked on with pride, as Dad leaned down and kissed her.
And that's the first time we saw,
"Our Little Sister."

The sweetest little gal, all ribbons and curls,
To us she was cuter than other little girls.
She could play with her brothers, and win every game.
With no hard feelings, they loved her the same.
Wherever she went, they went right along,
To them she couldn't do anything wrong.
We all spoiled her some, this sassy little miss,
It was natural for us, she was
"Our Little Sis."

She was always so full of vigor and vim,
Always looked on the bright side, never the grim.
She'd come bouncing in, with a great big smile,
Just happy and laughing all the while.
She'd enter the room and Mom's spirits would lift,
And she always brought some small token or gift.
Her Daddy too, could never resist her.
But we needed no excuse, she was "Our Little Sister."

As the years went by, all that changed was her name.
She had her own family, but was still the same.
She had a lot of good friends, some closer than others.
But she treated them all like her sisters and brothers.
She was a wife, a daughter, and a mother that's true,
And she was so proud, she was a Grandmother too.
All this she was, but "We" would like to list her,

First, last and always, she was
"Our Little Sister."

Yes, she's gone from Our world, God has called her away.
But we know we'll all see her again some day.
God has a plan for us being here on earth,
He knows our purpose, and he knows our worth.
He sent her to us for a while to love,
Then He called her back, to His Home up above.
While she was with us, she brought joy and bliss,
And we're glad he sent us,
"Our Little Sis."

I think I know now why he sent for her.
Letting us have her for such a short time, as it were,
He knew she'd worry about Mom and Dad when they've gone,
She'd be sad, and miss them through darkness and dawn.
So, to ease her pain and comfort her some,
He sent her ahead, to be there when they come.
And we won't be sad, even tho we've missed her,
She'll be waiting for us all,
"Our Little Sister."

Her life and her love we'll always remember,
Tho it be January, June or December.
We loved her then, and I'll tell you this,
We will love her forever,
"Our Little Sis."

In Loving Memory of Our Sister, Marion Lone McLean, Feb. 1, 1936-Sept. 6, 1977.
Written by Pearl Alfson [A Sister]

Tough Times – Wild Fire of 1988

September 1988 was hot and dry. I remember we had a group of eight guests in camp. At night we could see smoke and fire up Mineral Creek about 8 to 10 miles from camp. They were calling the fire "Canyon Creek Fire." It started in the Scapegoat Wilderness and headed towards our camp at Camp Creek. We quickly took our guests to the trailhead at Indian Meadows and sent out our packer Leon back to camp with mules to pick up leftover hay.

Jeff Hoeffner and a view of the Scapegoat Wilderness, ca. 1980s.

The Following day Kenny and Jeff checked with the Forest Service at the Lincoln Ranger District about the fire. They hoped to get them busy flying planes or anything to put the fire out. We knew with a little wind it might blow up! A couple of days later on September 6th it blew! Mineral Creek, along with our Meadow Creek Camp burned. Everything was lost. Hay, groceries, tents. It was all burned. It burned 280,000 acres in approximately twelve hours, all the way across the divide to Augusta. I wondered where the little bears went. Not up a tree I hope.

The Forest Service trail crew was working on the Middle Fork Trail camping out. Someone had to warn them, they had no clue! One of the rangers at the Forest Service, Jerry Burns, saddled a horse and headed into the wilderness. Fifteen miles up Middle Fork he finally found them. He and the crew cut the mules and horses loose and spent the night on Crow Peak in howling wind. The fire leapt from ridge to ridge, blowing debris and smoke. They watched as the fire blew across the mountain beneath them. They were lucky. The next morning a helicopter pulled them from atop of Crow Peak. Amazingly, their stock somehow survived.

Meadow Creek Camp before the Camp Creek Fire of 1988.

The K Lazy Three Outfitters Camp at Meadow Creek. The camp was completely destroyed by the Canyon Creek Fire of 1988.

Our camp at Meadow Creek on the East Fork of the North Fork of the Blackfoot River burned. We lost our large cook tent, wrangler tent, two sleeping tents, hay for hunting season, cooking utensils, corrals, everything. It was a sad sight. Tent frames burned, Dutch oven cracked, dead fish in the stream, burning logs everywhere. It was September 6, 1988, just before hunting season. We were in a tight spot, hunters coming and no camp! It was a great camp where Scotty Creek and Meadow Creek joined Bugle Mountain across the creek. What to do?

After the fire we had a meeting with the Forest Service. We were blessed to have great Forest Service rangers, Ernie Nunn and Jerry Burns, who let us pick a new camp on Meadow Creek. A beautiful camp next to Emerald Pool and Meadow Lake. The Forest Service helicoptered in equipment and let us use chain saws for a few days. We went to work borrowing tents and equipment. "Got er done!" We ordered a new cook tent and sleeping tent. By the second week in September we had hunters in camp. There were six or eight of them from North Carolina. They were repeat hunters, so they understood the situation. I remember I used to complain about wanting a new house! Kenny just said, "Don't complain, you get a new tent about every five years." I did love my new tents. Anyway, we put things together for the hunt and had one of the best seasons ever.

Tough Times – My Kenny

Oh, how we all miss him and his special laugh. I lost my Kenny in 1989 at age 56. He passed away in our old house from a heart attack. Jeff found him at home. Don, Ann, and Frank Martin took care of us during this sorrowful time and Art and Ruth Glaze helped also. Kenny was buried in Lincoln's old cemetery with a pack string on the headstone along with my name. We had wonderful, exciting years and a great family. Funeral was January 13, 1989. Community Hall was packed to overflowing. So much snow outside (three feet at the Lincoln Cemetery) that Dave Harrington and Mike Barthelmess hooked a team of white mules to a sleigh and put the casket on pine boughs. Noel and Brett Anderson plowed the cemetery road best they could. I wonder if I ever thanked them. I rode in the sleigh about a mile to the cemetery. The Lincoln Cemetery was founded in 1864 on a hillside above town. Groups of friends and relatives were there despite the cold weather. It was a little below zero that day. At the graveside, Jeff gathered the family in his arms and we all cried.

Everyone loved Kenny, loved his stories. He was very humorous with a quick wit and big laugh. He was an entertainer, and he worked hard. They always said he was the best timber faller in the valley. Could do anything and do it right. Packing or trucking, it didn't matter. The hunters and guides all thought the world of him.

Kenny Hoeffner enjoying a snowy day in the backcountry, ca. 1980s.

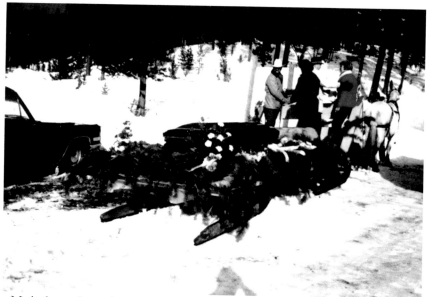

Mule drawn funeral procession for Kenneth R. Hoeffner, with Mike and Cindy Barthelmess, Dave Harrington, Russel Hoeffner, and Mary Faith Hoeffner.

The Hoeffner Family at the funeral of Kenneth R. Hoeffner. From left to right: Jeff, Judy, Jerrie, Mary Faith, Penny Jo, and Jackie.

Horses and Mules

We had wonderful horses over the years. We made them gentle with lots of miles. I put together a list of all the horses and mules I've had over the years. Some real good ones!

Coke – A ranch horse
Flash – A gold sorrel
Buckshot – Short, choppy buckskin
Little Buck – Jeff's buckskin
Patches – Kids' favorite
Beau – Small quarter horse everybody loved
Blaze – Beautiful palomino, a favorite
Sampson – Big sorrel
Duke – Bay quarter
Chief and Blue – They both bucked when we bought them, lots of miles, made them prize horses
Pike – Big sorrel
Cricket – Lots of heart
Will – Great wrangler horse
Fly – Regular quarter, Kenny's horse
Jerry – Belgium quarter
Johnny Walker – Walker horse
Coors – Big black walker
Deacon – Chestnut
Kid – Half quarter and Belgium mix
Spud – Belgium mix, also big horse and gentle
Ace and Duce – Two black percheron crosses, big and black

Most horses we bought around two years old and broke them. Generally, halter broke, tie to post and take a hind foot up with soft cotton rope and nobody gets kicked. Put a pack and saddle approximately 75 to 80 pounds to a side. Tie between two big mules and head down the trail. Maybe a few wrecks, but usually broke after a couple trips! Thirteen miles and that's the old way. Nowadays there are many new techniques. New round pens and even horse whisperers!

We also had many wonderful mules over the years. We started with seven big Belgian Cross mules. Kenny and I drove to Missouri for them. Great mules… after we got them broke. Had them many years. Here's a few more:

Amos and Andy – Bought as colts. Grew to be 17 hands. Big mules.
Kane and Able – Grulla mules
Kate and Ally – One black, one dun. Team mules for pulling wagon.
Buzz – Belgian quarter horse. Best elk packing mule you could ever have.

Soda – Good pack mule
Dewey – Belgian quarter horse mule, great meat mule.
Teton – Pack and ride mule
Molly – Pack and ride mule
Festus – Pack mule
Red – Good pack mule
Doc – My favorite riding mule
Squirrel – Little bay mule (watch her she kicks)

Mary Faith and a good riding mule, Molly.

Les Nader and I once drove to Springfield, Missouri, to pick up a load of mules. We hauled some cattle to New Mexico for the Mosher Ranch then picked up mules on the way home! Some white mules and my favorite mountain mule named Doc. Rode Doc in Jerrie's Arena in Helena with the barrel racers. Also rode him to Chinese Wall several times.

My Two Big Sorrel Horses

My two favorite mountain horses were Rooster and Macho. I'm not sure which was my favorite. Rooster was a top trail and wrangler horse. During hunting season, I would clean up my kitchen, get meat out for supper, bake a cake or cookies, and go hunting with Rooster. Sometimes we'd turn horses out at the corral, let them graze along Meadow Creek. I'd sit on my horse and watch them. So peaceful. The stock roamed around, picking out their favorite types of grass. There would usually be approximately ten head, mostly mules. They are all so playful and fun to watch. When they were full, they usually headed to the corral for horse pellets. We always fed horse pellets. It's a grain mixture and horses and mules love it.

I'd wrangle horses with Rooster up Camp Creek. We would start down the trail to find horses and he would sniff along the trail for horse scent, then stop and listen for horse bells. He could always find the horses. Once he got the scent or heard the bells you better be ready to ride because he could be a handful coming down off Camp Creek when chasing a horse. My good horse, Macho, was also a great wrangler. He was quick and could outrun almost anything. Macho was a great cow horse and was a registered quarter horse, grandson of The Ol' Man. He could cut a cow, not many got away from him. Darn sure I miss my old mountain horses. Put them down together here on the ranch across the meadow from the house in the big pine trees. I can almost see them standing over there swatting flies!

Weddings

With five children (four girls and one boy), there had to be weddings. Jackie, my oldest, married Gary Sparrow. Oh, how I remember. Their wedding was in our little church in Lincoln in July.

Her sisters were bridesmaids. We butchered a cow and had a big reception in the yard. There was a trellis over the gate painted white. We placed a big table against the old bunkhouse and loaded it with presents. The local ladies—Glazes, Andersons, Woods, and Helen Lundberg—all furnished huge salads. One of our favorite hunters from Texas even came. Our friends Bobby and Doris Winningham picked wildflowers and put them in tin cans for the picnic tables. Tons of food and fun! Beautiful wedding dress and beautiful bride. Jackie and Gary have two boys named Cody and K.C.

My second daughter, Jerrie, married a cowboy named Steve Downing in our little church. He was a bulldogger and real rodeo cowboy. He had two boys Luke and Kenny Downing, so Jerrie had her hands full. Steve was also a trucker. You know the song, "Mommas Don't Let Your Babies Grow Up to Be Cowboys." Especially with them darn trucks. Later they had Shawn and Desiree.

Desiree Downing, Jerrie Downing, and Shawn Downing, getting ready to head into the mountains.

Kenny and Mary Faith Hoeffner with their daughter Penny Jo at her wedding in Lincoln, Montana.

Left to right top: Penny Jo, Jeff, Mary Faith, Kenny, and Judy. Left to right: Jackie and Jerrie.

My third daughter, Judy, married Dave Morgan. Judy had a beautiful wedding dress and pastel bridesmaids' dresses. Judy and Dave Morgan were high school sweethearts and married in the church in Lincoln. We held the reception at the Seven Up Supper Club. Judy had a big beautiful hat and Dave, a cowboy guy, "wore out several saddles working for the Kern's Ranch." Judy's three sisters wore blue and pink bridesmaids' dresses. It was wonderful! Father Mac officiated. Judy had two children with Dave named Jessie and Mandy. Later, she married Phil Wirth and they have one son named Cody.

Penny Jo, our baby girl who helped us so much on pack trips, married Dan Quie from the trail crew. Penny Jo wore a beautiful dress and big hat. They married in our hayfield. Dan built a cross and we had hay bales for seats, even had a piano and horses in the field. Oh, it was a grand time. Dan's parents and three brothers dressed in white suites and Penny Jo's three sisters wore beautiful long dresses. Big reception in our yard. Dan's mom and dad loved the outdoor life also. Father Mac officiated for Penny Jo as well. He was our favorite priest. We all loved Father Mac. He died in a tragic kayaking accident on the Blackfoot River. Father Mac was a real outdoorsman. He once walked 14 miles to our camp to stay with us for a few days. In Helmville, they still have ceremonies for him. Everyone loved him.

We thought Jeff's would be an inexpensive wedding being a boy and all, but no! Jeff married Marie, the daughter of a Washington D.C. judge that visited our wilderness camps during the summer. They were married in Washington, D.C. We all flew back there. It was a beautiful wedding with a beautiful bride. We had a grand time with Marie's folks, Judge Jim Belson and Rosemary Belson. We toured Washington D.C. then everyone came back to Lincoln where we had a reception at the Seven Up Supper Club with friends and family. I now have three beautiful grandchildren: Colin, Kenny, and Caitlin. It was expensive, but worth it. It all started around a campfire at Meadow Creek.

5 KEEPING BUSY

My grandson, Jesse, and I were fishing on Meadow Creek I mentioned that I wanted to show him good fishing holes before I get old. Jesse said, "Grandma, you're already old." –Mary Faith Hoeffner

The Retirement Party

Because our outfitting license was under K Lazy Three Ranch, I was allowed to continue after Kenny's passing in 1989. Jeff and I worked together for ten more seasons 'til we decided to sell the business to Brett and Julie Todd. We led many pack trips down the trail, washed saddle blankets, oiled saddles, and wrangled horses, just the two of us We kept our brands, though. The K Lazy Three brand is on the left shoulder; the new K Lazy Three brand used by Brett and Julie Todd is on the right shoulder.

Mary Faith and Jeff Hoeffner at Indian Meadows with mules Cain and Abel, ca. 1990s.

In 1998 we sold our outfitting business to Brett Todd. No more driving teams or raising colts or pulling pack strings (or cooking). After we sold, the first thing I bought was a new Dodge half ton pickup and a four-horse trailer, a real cowgirl outfit. I also bought a

K⟋ RANCH

Outfitters · Guides

Phone (406) 362 4258
Lincoln, Montana 59639

Dear Friends:

Yes, we have sold our wilderness outfitting business!

We would sincerely like to thank all our friends -- old and new -- and the local businesses for their continued support during our 30-plus years in the outfitting business. It sure doesn't seem that long! It has been a business our family has thoroughly enjoyed.

We have made many friends along with having a wonderful outdoor experience, horses, mules, wildlife and wildflowers; not to mention "a few" mule wrecks, saddle sores, lost hunters and all the excitement that goes with it.

We would like to introduce the new owner, Brett Todd. Brett is a Montana Cowboy from Big Timber. He has a number of years experience in packing, guiding and ranching. He is a good hand. We know you will like him. Brett's family consists of wife, Julie and three children.

We hope you will continue with your support towards Brett and his new business, the K Lazy Three Ranch Inc.

Happy Trails.

> Mary Faith, Jeff
> and all the Hoeffner Family

Letter to friends and clients announcing the sale of K Lazy Three Outfitters and Guides, 1998.

new canvas tent. Why? I am not sure, guess I missed my tent in the mountains. I then drove to Grand Junction, Colorado; me, my two horses, and dog, Tango! My friend Phyllis Duvall had a job as a pool rider. I helped her keep track of 1,200 head of cows on top of the Grande Mesa National Forest. We lived in an old-line shack amid the quaking aspens. Not much cooking or cleaning! Up in the morning, coffee, pull on boots, catch a horse and head out. Beautiful country with cows and no fences.

I stayed with Phyllis for two weeks then drove to Buena Vista Colorado and stayed with Jackie, my eldest daughter. We rode out on the high desert across the headwaters of the Arkansas River. New country and good horses; Bailey, Rooster, and dog, Tango. After visiting Jackie, I drove to Dillon, Montana, where Jerrie met me and we drove to Butte. It was Labor Day weekend. Rodeo at Helmville, so we stopped and watched the rodeo. Then on home. What a super couple of weeks.

After I got back we decided on a retirement party for me. The Forest Service gave me a set of Forest Service dishes: plates and cups. It's a set, for my thirty years of service as an outfitter in the National Forest. It was winter; lots of snow. Invited everyone: relatives, friends, and the Forest Service. We had the party in our back meadow among the tall ponderosa pines across the meadow from the house. Snow was deep, so we built a huge bonfire, had hamburgers plus a potluck lunch. Hooked up our team of mules to the ol' hayrack with pine boughs and hauled guests from the old house to the meadow. Leon Meuchel had his team, so we had two teams hauling back and forth plus some sleigh rides in the meadows. Many friends came on snowmobiles. It was a huge party! The hay meadow was alive with people. Liz and Jerry Cain, the Glazes, the Andersons, and several others sang songs with us late into the night. We sang every kind of song we could think of. What a fun party.

Wrecked My New, White Chevy Pickup

It wasn't too long after I retired that I went to Helena to visit some of my kids. Had a meeting to get to in the evening, but somebody had to get home to feed the horses in Lincoln. That would be me! So, I got in my new, white Chevy pickup and headed for Lincoln. I was traveling maybe a little fast! Headed up Flesher Pass and came around a corner and hit a bunch of sheet ice. My pickup spun around and headed off the side of the road into a steep canyon. Trees down both sides. The pickup kinda stopped on the edge and teetered there thinking about tipping over the edge. I remember thinking "It's not going over." But it did. Straight down with me and my dog, Tuffy, sitting on the seat next to me. It was like riding a bumper car hitting one tree, then the next. "When is this pickup going to hit a tree and stop?" I thought.

Well it finally did. We slammed into a tree and a big limb busted the window on the driver side. I thought about what to do. "Well," I thought. "The sanding crew will be along, just wait 'til they find me and Tuffy in the morning." Finally, I heard a voice say, "Is there anybody down there?" I said, "Yes, could you give me a hand?" The fellow started down, but the hillside was so steep and icy that he fell and slid down to the pickup. He helped me get out the side door and me and Tuffy walked up the mountain on a game trail.

A neighbor from Lincoln gave me a ride back to Helena to Jerrie's to call Jeff and my insurance agent. My lip was bleeding. I must have hit my mouth on the steering wheel. Jerrie took me to the emergency room for stitches and Jeff and our friend, Terry Dunlap, drove up Flesher Pass to where the pickup plunged off the road. They had to get a wrecker to pull it up the mountain. I remember the wrecker driver saying, "You musta had an angel on your shoulder." It was a major accident. Totaled my new pickup! Jeff and Terry just shook their heads. Jeff said, "Mom, you're very lucky, it coulda' been the end." I didn't get to the meeting that evening. Don't know who fed the horses.

Best Friends: A Couple Good Dogs

Oh, how can I say it? We had lots of different dogs at different times, but my really close partners were Tango, Tuffy, and Toby. Tango was a beautiful border collie and Australian shepard mix. Black with a white collar. Someone gave him to Jeff, but he ended up at my house as my dog! This dog went with me everywhere. One time he was chasing a bunch of horses in the pasture in Augusta and they bunched up and ran over him and broke his leg. We had a cast put on and he ran 12 miles with us on pack trips. He slept under my cot in the cooking tent in camp for many years. When I flew out on the helicopter with my broken leg, one of the guides had to rope him and drag him out from under the cot in the cooking tent. I guess he missed me. I had him for twelve years.

Tuffy was my little black dog. My faithful companion for eleven years. I remember when he was a puppy—a little black ball of fur. He had a snip of white on his head and neck, so white that you could see him coming towards you, especially at night running down the road. I remember when I first got him. I would walk up, keep cool, and put him inside my jacket. Gradually he ran alongside me. He chased cows with me at Lewis and Clark Trail Ranch. Always right out there moving cows or running along the corral chutes, biting at cows. He went with me in the mountains to Webb Lake and Heart Lake running along the trail, over logs, yet he never seemed to get tired. One time I told him to stay at the horse trailer, but he came along behind. His little short legs kept him busy. He was tough.

Tuffy always entertained himself picking up pinecones or sticks; rolling in the snow. Oh, I miss him. I really miss him. He chased the horses for me. They respected him. I would say, "Get those horses," and like a little black streak away he went. However, he wouldn't chase the buckskin. He hated the buckskin and the buckskin hated him. The buckskin would chase him with both front feet slapping the ground. Then he would turn and Tuffy would be after him, nipping his heels.

Tuffy even went to church we me. He sat in the car for hours at Walmart waiting for me. He was a border collie/corgi mix. Everyone loved him. At the rodeo grounds they all knew Tuffy. One day we were on the golf cart at the Lincoln ranch and I turned a fast corner and he fell off. When I harrowed the field, he would lay out in the field until I finished. Sometimes I would hardly know he was there. Wake up in the morning, open the door, and in came Tuffy. He always wanted his belly scratched. Should have appreciated him more. My little black dog with short legs and white feet. He was one of a kind. Never to be replaced.

After Tuffy was killed in an accident, a friend found me a new dog. I am just lost without a dog. The dog's name was Toby. I just loved him from the start. A little brown and white half corgi, half Queensland heeler mix. Weighed about 35 pounds. He took to me right away. By my side all the time. Learned to open my garage door by jumping above the latch and pushing open the door. Loved to be on my bed and chase the football and bring it back to me. A natural herding dog, brought the horses in. They didn't mess with him. He was very aggressive.

They called him an Australian cattle dog, bred to herd cattle in the Australian Outback. Oh, I loved that little dog, but he liked to chase anything that moved, like Jeff's two peacock hens. He killed them when he was just a pup. We sat up on the mountain, me and Toby. His head always in my lap, watching for when the cows came over the mountain. He bristled up and growled. He was my protector. I sent him after the cows and he went barking and moved them. Toby met with a tragic horse accident that killed him. A horse struck him on the head. I was devastated. I am at a loss. I can never replace that type of dog.

Mary Faith (riding Rooster) with two of her favorite dogs, Tango and Tuffy.

My Cowgirl Friends

I had many wonderful cowgirl friends over the years. They are some of the best women I know.

Amy Haverland accompanied me on many wagon rides down the trails to Arrasta Creek and to Indian Meadows.

Cheryl Heppner hales from Lincoln. We rode together a bunch. Friend and helper. Rode an Appaloosa horse.

Cindy Meilar, a Browning cowgirl who moved to Lincoln. She would ride anything with hair. Fun days, barrels and poles. Rode to

North Cabin and wrangled cows at Lewis and Clark Ranch and the Lincoln Rodeo Association.

Jackie, my cowgirl daughter, rode with me in Colorado and Arizona.

Jerrie, my cowgirl daughter, rode with me at the Wickenburg, Arizona, rodeo where she barrel raced. She sold and trained barrel horses. Jerrie rode many trails with me. Remember Jerrie and a friend riding into camp one fall with two feet of snow on the ground and temperature at 30 below zero. A 13-mile ride. I rode to Parker Lake to meet them. Lucky they made it.

Judy, my cowgirl daughter, rode too, and helped me cook and hunt. She was with me when I shot my goat.

Penny Jo, my daughter, loved to ride. A darn good rider too! Any time, any place. She gathered cows on Lewis and Clark Trail Ranch and cooked for one season at the outfitting camp. She brought me back from Wickenburg, Arizona, one year.

Lola May and Sarah Jane, two of my favorite people. Went on summer pack trips with me. From Missoula. Went on the ladies rides with me. When I was sick they met me in Missoula and had lunch with me.

Melinda Ridge from Thomasville, North Carolina, came on a fishing trip with her husband, but stayed with me for a ladies' ride up Sun River Canyon. Melinda with her long fingernails! She said she was going to teach me to be a southern lady. I said I was going to teach her to be a cowgirl. Sure loved her accent.

Nancy Anderson was from Colville, Washington. Met her in Lincoln. Rode for the Grazing Association. She would gather cows at Lewis and Clark Trail Ranch. Went to Mexico and Arizona with me. Fun, fun!

Nancy Brady, a real Texas cowgirl. Went on ladies' rides and wagon train rides with me. She brought her horse, saddle, horse trailer, and away we went, backcountry or whatever. She also helped with the cattle at Lewis and Clark Trail Ranch.

Nancy Klick, my sister from Augusta. She and her husband Dick Klick owned the K-L Ranch up Sun River Canyon. My sister Nancy was a high school rodeo queen and loved to ride up High Trail around Gibson Dam.

Phyllis Duvall from Colorado. She was a pool rider, roped, and doctored cows. Had approximately 1,200 head to watch on the Grand Mesa National Forest. She was also an endurance rider and cattle boss in Colorado. Gathered cows on Lewis and Clark Trail Ranch and packed into the mountains with me.

Susie and Chris Gehring, my rancher friends from across the river. I loved their dogs and favorite cowboy horse. Helped them gather and sort cows many times. In return, they helped me cook in camp. We had a great time. I always took potato salad for them when they were branding.

Viola Thomas hails from Canada. A real hand! Raised paint horses and trained rodeo horses. She's quite a horse trader. Hazed for bulldogged horses and rode racehorses (and trained them too). Rodeo, pack strings, what have you. She did it all.

More Friends

Lou and Henry Darr were originally from North Carolina and came out and hunted for ten or twelve years with us. They went on summer trips with us to the Chinese Wall. They bought a ranch in Helmville, Montana, and became our dear friends. I went to visit them in North Carolina several times. Great friends through the years!

Sharon and Kenny White were great friends! Helped us when we were just starting out with the business and when we lived in Augusta. Sharon and Kenny helped us set camp and guided for us. Cutting trails or hunting, they did it all. Met in Augusta and stayed friends forever. Sharon went with me on many trips and helped cook. Kenny went on summer trips with their boys Steve and Jeff White. Many adventures through the years!

Mary Faith and Macho at a Fourth of July Parade in Lincoln, Montana.

83rd birthday party for Mary Edna Faith Mills McLean. From left to right: Kenny McLean (brother), Nancy Klick (sister), JoAnne Jerome (sister), Stephen McLean (brother), Mary Edna Faith Mills McLean (mother), Mary Faith Hoeffner.

My New House

It was one of those darn cold winters in Lincoln after Kenny had passed. Jeff came to the house to thaw out the water line under the house again. With no crawl space, it was a challenge! The water pipes froze every winter for many years. We would thaw them out, and cuss, then spring came and you'd forget about it for another year.

Jeff was the only one thin enough to get under the house to work on the pipes. He came over with a friend, Terry Dunlap, a builder from Helena. Terry said, "Darn it, Jeff, your mother needs a new house, and I could build her one." So, he did. It was hard to heat that old house. It had sawdust insulation in the walls and a dirt roof over the living room. Nice for cats, though. It was cold and a hundred years old. So, Terry built me a new house back where the timber meets the meadow facing Stonewall Mountain. We decided to rent out the old ranch house. I love my new house! No more frozen water pipes. Best decision I ever made.

Tough Times 2011 – Ranch House Burned Down

Snowing, April 7, 2011, 10:00 pm. I looked across the white meadow and saw smoke rising from the old ranch house. I drove to check on it and found a fire crew there along with my renters. They, of course, were upset. All their belongings were inside. They assumed it wouldn't burn. Lots of sawdust in the walls and newspaper for insulation, though.

I returned to my new house across the meadow, watched out the window. More smoke. House in huge flames, burning like a big bonfire. Flames and sparks high into the black night. So many memories in the fire and smoke. Two of my children, Penny Jo and Jeff, were born there. Kenny passed there. Many fun times with neighbors and kids. Big beautiful lawn and big, tall ponderosa pine trees. My grandmother's lilac bushes, bonfire pit, so many Fourth of July birthday parties, weddings, all my kids grew up there. I watched it all from my window across the meadow.

The house is gone now. Stood there one hundred and six years. It was made of big logs, about 24 inches in diameter. Had a sod roof and homestead room 16 by 20 feet, with kitchen and bed and bath added alongside. Wood cook stove and barrel heating stove. Time flies! Just the other day I looked out across the meadow. I was very sad, then thought to myself, "That ol' house was tired." You know, it was ready to go!

First and Last Pack Trip

I remember Gene and Martha Youdarian, local outfitters and wonderful friends. They took me on my very first pack trip from Indian Meadow Trailhead to Basin Creek. Two nights on the trail. What a trip! We packed in everything for their hunting camp: groceries, tents, stoves, etc. Three big strings of eight mules, 80 pounds to a side.

After that trip I was hooked on the wilderness, the mountains, the streams, the trails. When Gene passed, I packed his wife, Martha, and daughter, Becky, into camp with Gene's ashes. Martha, Phyllis, and Becky rode to Crow Creek on a cold and windy day and scattered the ashes at Gene's old camp. He took me on my first pack trip, and I took him on his last.

Wagon Rides

Some of my fondest memories with friends and family are from our wagon rides. Three days and three nights, 60 miles, Sucker Creek to Augusta. I was in my seventies, but that's okay. Up over the Continental Divide we'd climb. Ten wagons and 60 to 70 riders. We started at Sucker Creek in Lincoln. Teams and riders saddle up! Nancy Brady rode Macho and me on Rooster. Traveled to Lewis and Clark Ranch. Camped near Krone Lake. When in camp, unsaddle and put up the tent. Horses tied on high line. What a sight to see those twenty horses on the high line! Macho and Rooster were used to it, so no problem.

Next day they took us across Lewis and Clark Trail, the same one the Indians used. You can see their marks over the pass. A friend of mine drove my mules, Kate and Allie. It was a big and long pull for the mules with the wagon. We had to get a couple cowboys to hook on the tongue of the wagon and help pull. Leon Meuchel drove his team of horses, and Stan and Peggy Reverts drove their big black mules. Not everyone could drive them. They were powerful mules. Over the divide we went. Beautiful scenery! We could see all the way to Great Falls and over into Blackfoot Valley.

Driving down was tricky over boulders and ruts. Hard on mules and horses with wagons pushing on them. Use your wagon brake if you had one! I rode along the wagon and Stan and Peggy said, "You look a little tired." It was a long day. Stan hollered, "Mary Faith, tie your horse to the back of our wagon and ride along and drink whiskey with me and Peggy." So I did!

Looking out the back of a wagon on a ride through the Blackfoot River Valley with Nancy Brady (left) and Mary Faith (center).

We camped across the divide. Meals were catered, so throw out your sleeping bag and get supper. Wonderful meals provided by local ladies. Leon kept telling stories in the evening and shoeing horses for some without shoes. Leon did a wonderful job reciting "The Cremation of Sam McGee." Up the next morning with ham, scrambled eggs, and pancakes on the menu. Pick up your lunch and get on your horse. Last night we camped near Bear Lake then onto the dusty trail. Need a spit bath! Rode on into Augusta for a big BBQ and dance. Great times! I went on four wagon rides over the years: The Highwoods, Sun River, Stanford, and Lincoln. Took my mules Kate and Ally on three rides. New country on good horses! Many good friends. What more could you ask for?

Wickenburg, Arizona

The Stevensons and I met Penny and Sid Arthur, a young couple who loved cow sorting, at the McFarland Arena in Wickenburg, Arizona, and they let me and my horse tag along to horse races in Phoenix, Arizona. There I met Tad and Susie Mills. Tad was a horse trader cowboy, roper, and story teller. They have an arena at Congress, Arizona. Susie, a wonderful team roper and friend. Some of us greenhorns tried roping. Oh yes, guess I did heel a couple of little donkeys while there. Just a fun place to spend a sunny afternoon, drink a cool beer, and ride some horses. I rode my gray horse, Profit.

I heard so much about Wickenburg, Arizona, that I made arrangements for me and my horse and went and stayed with the Stevensons for a month. Rented a camper and corrals, rode on the desert. Next year we went for two months. Enjoyed the weather and riding, but not the rattlesnakes. My kids, Jackie, Jerrie, Judy, Penny Jo, and Jeff, each visited me and took a turn driving me to Wickenburg, Arizona.

Jerrie, my second daughter, the barrel racer, took her horse and competed and won the Wickenburg rodeo. We rented a big house together. She barrel raced and I sorted cows. Kept my horse at Horsepitality! Met lots of wonderful cowgirls.

Grandkids and Turkeys

Grandkids, oh yes! All ages and all very athletic. Into basketball, football, and cowboys. Swimmers, ropers, bulldoggers, barrel racers, horse trainers, saddle bronc riders, and ranchers! They are so fun to watch grow up. The family will be here for Thanksgiving so better buy a big turkey I cooked a turkey for each hunt in the wilderness for years. Hunters loved it, but by the time Thanksgiving rolled around, cooking another turkey was not too exciting!

Mary Faith with grandchildren Caitlin, Colin, and Kenny Hoeffner at Arrasta Creek Trailhead.

It's Not Over Yet

The Lincoln ranch has been here for over a hundred years! It's seen a lot of history during that time. I plan to continue living there as long as possible. The ranch will go to my children and grandchildren if my future plans continue. It's now October 2014 as I finish up this memoir about my life. Outside across the meadow the aspen are turning yellow. Here I am still on the ranch with three horses I raised and trained. Rode up on the Elkhorn Mountains last week chasing cattle with my son Jeff, and grandson Colin, and two cowboys, David Clark and Jim Stein. We rode to the top of the mountain where I decided to sit in the sun and wait for the cows to come down the ridge. Sitting on the very top of the Elkhorn Mountains just me and my horse and dog, Toby. Life couldn't be better and it's not over yet!

Mary Faith and her horses Badger, Profit, and Sister at the Lincoln Ranch, October, 2014.

6 REMEMBERING MOM AND DAD

Mary Faith Hoeffner Obituary

Mary Faith at age 81 riding Profit and leading Badger during a branding.

Mary Faith Hoeffner - Montana rancher, wilderness outfitter, and beloved wife and mother - passed away peacefully on Monday, October 12, 2015, at the age of 83 at her home in Lincoln, surrounded by her family.

Mary Faith was born in Great Falls on April 24, 1932, to L. Kenneth and Faith Mills McLean. She grew up on a ranch near Fairfield where, as the first-born child, she was her father's "right-hand man," assisting with the cattle, calving, haying, and performing the many chores a ranch girl of the mid 1900s was expected to do.

The family moved to Augusta in 1948 where they purchased a ranch where they raised Polled Hereford cattle and sold registered bulls. Mary

Faith graduated from Augusta High School in 1950, where she played basketball and was a cheerleader. She was also a member of the first Montana High School Rodeo Team and won the barrel racing event at the state rodeo in Augusta. She was also an accomplished trick rider and performed at rodeos and cattle sales throughout the state. She attended Montana State College where she was a member of the rodeo team.

In 1952, Mary Faith married the cowboy of her dreams, Kenneth R. Hoeffner, and together they raised five children: Jackie, Jerrie, Judy, Penny Jo, and Jeff. She always wanted to live close to the mountains and when the opportunity arose in 1959 they purchased a small ranch in Lincoln. Their love for fishing and hunting inspired her and Kenny to start the K Lazy Three Ranch, an outfitting and guide service. They guided hunters and fishermen in the Scapegoat Wilderness for more than 30 years. All five children were very involved in the success of this business as well as being "on call" for their mom throughout her life. After Kenny passed away in January 1989, Mary Faith and her son, Jeff, operated the business together for 10 more seasons. She was a longtime member of the Montana Outfitters and Guides Association, the Ladies Auxiliary and the Lincoln Rodeo Club.

If her many friends couldn't find her on her tractor harrowing or working on her beautiful flower beds, Mary Faith could most likely be found riding one of her many good horses down a mountain trail with her beloved dog by her side.

She was recently working on her book, *Nothing Like Riding a Good Horse in New Country: This is My Story as I Remember*, where she shares her memories, adventures and challenges of being one of Montana's few women outfitters. This quote from the book sums up the fulfilling life she led: "They say every woman needs a good man, a good horse, and a good dog. Guess I've had them all!" Mary Faith was a devoted mother and grandmother, and thoroughly enjoyed sharing her love for horses with her grandchildren. She also took great interest in their accomplishments and activities.

Grandchildren in order of age right to left at the funeral of Mary Faith Hoeffner. Luke Downing, Kenny Downing, Cody Sparrow, Brooke Quie, Jesse Morgan, K.C. Sparrow, Shawn Downing, Mandy Morgan, Desiree Downing McFadden, Kari Quie, Kelly Quie, Colin Hoeffner, Kenny Hoeffner, Cody Wirth, Caitlin Hoeffner. Cody Sparrow and Brooke Quie were honored to speak at Mary Faith's funeral, October, 2015.

The riderless horse at the funeral of Mary Faith Hoeffner. From left to right: Jesse Morgan, Colin Hoeffner, Caitlin Hoeffner, and Kenny Hoeffner, October, 2015.

In addition to her husband, Mary Faith was preceded in death by a sister, JoAnne McLean in 2014. She is survived by her five children, Jackie Sparrow of Buena Vista, CO, (Gary); Jerrie (Downing) Dolan, of East Helena, (Don); Judy Wirth of Wolf Creek, (Phil); Penny Jo Quie, of Elk River, MN; and Jeff Hoeffner, of Winston, MT, (Marie); and grandchildren, Cody and KC Sparrow; Shawn Downing and Desiree McFadden; Luke and Kenny Downing; Jesse Morgan, Mandy Sunford and Cody and Mike Wirth; Brooke, Kari and Kelly Quie; Colin, Kenny and Caitlin Hoeffner; and many great grandchildren and one great-great grandchild; as well as, sister, Nancy Klick of Augusta; Kenneth McLean of Sumner, WA (Jean); and Stephen McLean of Anacortes, WA (Elizabeth); and numerous nieces and nephews.

The entire Hoeffner family at Mary Faith's funeral, October, 2015.

Kenneth R. Hoeffner Obituary

Kenneth R. Hoeffner, 56, of Lincoln, died Friday at his home of an apparent heart attack. He had been a hunting and fishing outfitter and guide for the past 22 years in the Lincoln area. He was born July 25, 1932, in Great Falls, to the late John E. and Alberta F. Hoeffner. He grew up in Carter, where he went to the Knees School until moving to Fort Benton and later Augusta, where he finished his schooling. On

May 10, 1952, he married Mary Faith McLean, formerly of Augusta, in Denver, Colo. He served four years in the U.S. Air Force, where he was a gunner on a B-29 during the Korean War. Upon his discharge, he returned to Augusta and later to Fairfield. He moved to Lincoln in 1958. He owned and operated a ranch there and started an outfitting business, which he operated until the time of his death.

Mr. Hoeffner was active in various community affairs in Lincoln, was commander of the VFW Post No. 3369 in 1963 and 1964, and served as president of the Professional Wilderness Outfitters Association. He was a member of MOGA. He was an avid outdoorsman and enjoyed hunting, fishing and snowmobiling, according to his family. Survivors include his wife, Mary Faith of Lincoln; four daughters, Jackie Sparrow of Troy, Jerrie Downing and Judy Morgan, both of Helena, and Penny Jo Quie of Elk River, Minn.; one son, Jeff Hoeffner of Lincoln; one brother, Russell Hoeffner of Ceylon, Minn; and 11 grandchildren. He was preceded in death by his parents and a brother.

Rosary will be recited at the St. Jude Catholic Church in Lincoln. Mass of the resurrection will be celebrated Tuesday at 11:00 a.m. from St. Jude Catholic Church with the Rev. William J. Greytak officiating. Casket bearers will be Frank Martin, Art Glaze, Kevin Cole, Les Nader, Don Martin, Kenny White and Ward Kemmer. Honorary casket bearers will be Dick Klick, Dick Robinson, Jerry Jerome, Steven and Ken McLean-and Buster Robinson. Military graveside services will be at the Lincoln Cemetery. Hagler-Anderson Mortuary is in charge of arrangements.

Mary Faith's hat, chaps, and manti ropes, hanging from a branch somewhere in the backcountry.

Sharing Memories:
A Few Thoughts by Mary Faith and Kenny's Children

Jackie

Our mom, I sometimes wonder why we were so lucky (my sisters and brother) to have our mom. She wasn't an average mom, but someone so unique. I never appreciated my mom until I was older. As I watched how she lived her life, my mother became my hero. She was a tough act to follow, and we all wanted to live up to her expectations. And, they were HIGH. I remember the backcountry and all the fun we had, how she rode 14 miles each way in and out of the backcountry, sometimes in freezing cold, wind, and rain, summer trips and hunting trips. She loved packing and planning meals, horses, and showing everyone a good time in the wilderness. One summer mom and dad took all of us kids and grandkids for a fishing trip. I realize now what a lot of work that was, and my kids, Cody Sparrow and K.C. Sparrow still remember it. They loved to ride with Mary Faith at the ranch.

One of my favorite times with my mother was in Wickenburg, Arizona, where she stayed for three months every winter with her horse, of course! I flew to Phoenix in February to visit and enjoy some sunshine. Mom and my sister, Jerrie, picked me up. The talk on the way to Wickenburg was horses, horses, horses! Now, I like horses, but not like my sister and mom. I felt a little out of my element. I started wondering why did I come here? Guess it's not to lie in the sun drinking margaritas. It's going to be dusty corrals, grooming horses, and flies!

Mom was 80 years old at the time and looked like someone in her late fifties, and in better shape than I was. She boarded her horse in a horse motel about twenty minutes away from where she was staying. The next morning, we were up by 6:00 am, fixed breakfast and headed to the horse motel to take care of her horse. She did this every day.

Every morning by 8am she'd spent two hours feeding, watering, cleaning out the pen, getting hay and feed, etc. She'd visit with all the friends she had made who were there doing the exact same thing. Everyone knew mom, and they respected her. "Okay," I thought. This isn't so bad after all. Most days we would bathe the horse and she would work the horse in the round pen for about an hour. I got tired just watching her. No wonder she was in such good shape. The horse she had raised from a colt and trained herself. It was well behaved and well loved. It knew who was the boss. Mom knew what she was doing.

Jackie and Mary Faith with Tango at the old ranch house in Lincoln, Montana.

Every evening at 5:00 pm we were back down at the horse motel taking care of the horse. Usually one of us would take a little ride that evening. Mom had planned something for me to do every day I was there. A day ride with two of her cowboy friends; we packed lunches and brought along lots of water. It was a beautiful ride in the desert. Mom loaded up her horse two different days and we went to her team pinning competition. There were about twenty teams competing and I sat on the fence and watched her compete. She seemed at ease and confident on her horse. Sitting well in the saddle they say. She was a cowgirl, jeans, hat, and boots all clean and crisp! I was so proud of her. She usually placed in the top ten.

Later on in the week, I watched her ride in her cowgirl drill team. They had been practicing for weeks. This was the grand finale. It was held in a huge arena at the horse motel. Twenty cowgirls, music, matching shirts and hats. It was awesome. Mom was by far the oldest cowgirl there (but you couldn't tell by looking at her) and the best rider. Afterwards there was a picnic and homemade ice cream. I was having fun in spite of myself.

Mom also planned a trip with my sister, Jerrie, to take a canyon ride for a day. We drove the horses about thirty minutes out of Wickenburg and rode through an incredible canyon for miles. It was great fun. She wanted to show me a good time, and she did. On Sunday we went to the Cowboy Church where she knew everyone. Back in Buena Vista, Colorado, where I live, one of the church groups came into the restaurant I manage. I overheard them talking about an amazing cowgirl they met in Wickenburg, Arizona. I later found out it was mom they were talking about. It's a small world!

Before I knew it, my week was up and I was on my way home, wishing I could have stayed longer. I had such a good time. Our mom was one tough lady, the real deal as they say. She could be your best friend or your worst nightmare! We have all been blessed by having her in our lives, teaching us to be true to ourselves. She taught us to try new things and to find and live our passion, like she did.

Jerrie

All of us kids worked in the Bob Marshall Wilderness camps at one time or another. On hunting trips, when a hunter bagged an elk, the elk was quartered out and the quarters were tied high up on a pole between two trees we called an "elk pole." The meat was hung on the elk pole to keep it from grizzly bears, which were plentiful in the Bob Marshall. Tying the elk up high didn't stop the bears, so bells were hung on the elk quarters. If a bear could get to the meat, the bells would ring and alert the hunters to go run the bear off.

I remember being on one trip, which I now refer to as the night of the grizzly. We had only been in camp a couple of days and the hunters had already shot two nice bull elk. We woke up one morning to find that an elk quarter was missing from the elk pole and the bells, well, they were no match for the rugged mountain we had climbed and the celebration and late-night stories of a successful hunting trip. On further investigation, mom and dad found bear tracks, and they weren't small. This was one big bear! The next night we were ready. We all slept with one eye open, knowing a bear, possibly a grizzly was close by, and had already been rewarded for his cunning efforts once. We were certain he would be back for more. That night, however, was quiet and we were all relieved we hadn't been awakened by an unwelcome visitor.

Jerrie and Mary Faith at a Fourth of July parade in Lincoln, Montana.

Dad was always the first to get up and put the coffee on in the morning. He'd then venture out of the tent to check things out. On his morning round he was not surprised to find that another elk quarter was missing. The hunters, on the other hand, couldn't believe it. Some of them had bear permits that had yet to be filled, and here a big bear had snuck in right under their noses to share in their hard-earned prize.

The next night the hunters had big plans to stay up all night to catch the dirty mongrel stealing their elk. They even added a few more cow bells to the elk pole. However, after a long hard day of hunting combined with cards, campfire, and some strong drink (and, of course, listening to bear stories), the hunters soon gave up and burrowed down deep into their sleeping bags. Meanwhile, in the cook tent, I was the unlucky one who got to sleep on a cot next to the stove. My job at night was to keep the fire going. When I woke up shivering I knew it was time to put another log on the fire. Mom and dad slept in a different area of the same tent. When you're in the tent housing all the food, food that bears are great at sniffing out, and you know there is a big bear, possibly a grizzly, looking for dinner, you don't get much sleep. That was the case this night. Every time the wind moved the tent flaps it made my eyes snap open. The crack of a branch would make every muscle in my body tense up and my heart pound. We all lay there, mom, dad, and I, half asleep; then it happened … the cow bells rang.

We all heard it at once and shot straight up out of bed. Without saying a word, mom grabbed the lantern and dad grabbed the gun he kept beside his bed. Dad opened the tent flap to walk out and saw the bear lumbering toward the open tent flap. All at once mom grabbed ahold of the tent flap, dad's 30-06 rang out, and the bear turned straight away and was gone. Mom quickly lit the lantern; we all took a deep breath to assess the situation. The hunters were sitting straight up on their cots, just as scared stiff as I was. Dad notified them that he had shot the bear, but didn't know if he had killed it. They went out with flashlights but came back empty handed. That night was tense. An injured bear of any kind is a heck of a lot more aggressive than a healthy one. None of us slept the rest of that morning.

When the sun came up it was business as usual, but everyone was on edge. If we didn't find a dead bear it would be safe to assume there was an angry one close by. Later that morning, after scouring the surrounding brush, they did find a big grizzly. Turns out the shot was fatal and a big grizzly lay not 300 yards form camp.

I watched my mom and followed her cues on how to handle the situation. She was such a strong woman, and so brave. To me, she never seemed scared, even though I know she had to have been. She always just did what needed to be done and never complained.

She is so missed! When I think of my mom, the phrase "Never look back" is the first thing that comes to mind. That phrase fit her from the earliest memories and lasted to the end of her life. It's not just a maxim for how she lived her life, it's also literally how she did everything. If you were behind her you better keep up or you might be left behind or lost, just like the Tennessee Walker bred horses she liked to ride in the backcountry. When she moved, it was with haste and purpose. She told me when she was sad or down about something, her mother, Faith Mills McLean, would say, "Go wash your face and hands, comb your hair, put on a pressed white shirt, and you'll feel better." I remember her doing just that, and she always gave me the same advice, to this day it still works.

Judy

Judy and Mary Faith on a fall ride to Heart Lake in the Bob Marshall Wilderness.

I have many memories of the mountains. I realize now how lucky I was to have the opportunity to have the time back in the Scapegoat and Bob Marshall Wildernesses. I remember us kids riding our horses bareback to Twin Lakes and going out on the lake all day on the old rafts, then riding back to camp at dark. I am not sure how many of us really knew how to swim.

After I graduated from high school, I decided to stay home and help mom and dad. There was a lot that went on that year. In the mornings we would go wrangle the horses for the day. We always had people wanting hourly horseback rides. Us kids would take them out for rides; we had a trail around the ranch. Whichever of us kids needed the money the most was usually the one willing to take them. One morning dad and I went to wrangle the horses for the day. We rode all over the pasture and couldn't find the horses. So, we decided to ride down by the river. There they were, our twelve horses lying dead on the riverbank. That was a shocking sight to see. We lost some good horses. Most of the horses we had had for years. You really got attached to each horse. That was our parent's livelihood. I will never forget the look on my dad's face. Then we had to go tell mom. That evening, needless to say, dad had a few toddies. The state of Montana had an autopsy done on the horses. The Lincoln community held a benefit for our family.

That hunting season mom and I were up every morning at 3:00 am making breakfast and sack lunches for the hunters. We wanted to have them on top of the mountain by daybreak. Then, after they were sent off, mom and I would head out hunting. We tracked a lot of elk, but never got one. I haven't really been a hunter, but mom had always loved to hunt. I remember tracking one elk and we went a long way thinking we were getting close, never did, and it was a long way back to the horses. That year mom got her mountain goat. Dad, Dan Quie, and I were with her when she shot her goat. She shot the goat on Lost Pony. That was a fun experience. Glad I was with her.

One thing I remember about the hunters was how much they appreciated everything. It was such a new experience for them. I think a lot of the hunters just liked being away from their phones. Dad told a lot of good stories. Mom always said dad's stories changed. Mom cooked a lot of good food. One thing that sticks in my mind that mom told me was that you have to keep moving or you'll die. She kept moving!

Penny Jo

I was trying to think of a story when I was in camp with mom. I remember one that seems to always end the same, with her getting to fly out in a helicopter and the rest of us having to ride out in the cold. We were at camp for hunting season, and mom wanted to get out and go hunting. She loved to do that. I think she went up Bugle Mountain, so dad and I stayed in camp. Dad was in the cook tent and I was in the sleeping tent. The rest of the hired hands were out with the hunters.

I heard a sound like a horse coming across the creek. So, I ran down to the corrals and found mom's horse with the reins hanging down and her gun still fastened to the saddle. I ran up to the cook tent and told dad. He went down to the corral, jumped on mom's horse, and went across the creek. He found mom stumbling down the mountain. She had lost her glasses and couldn't see a thing. She had blood running down her face. He brought her back, and we put her on the bed. Every time she coughed, more blood would run out of the hole in her head. There was blood everywhere.

Mary Faith, Jackie, and Penny Jo at the Lincoln Ranch.

Jeff rode out to get help. Dad and I went down a little past the corral and made a big X for the helicopter to find. When the helicopter arrived, dad went with mom, and I stayed in camp. I remember well when Dan, one of the guides, came back to camp a little tipsy and a bit late. Dan and some of the hunters had stopped by another hunting camp. I was so mad because I had just cleaned up the mess and was worried about mom. I went with Dan to the corral to feed the horses and he couldn't tell one end of a horse form the other. One nice thing about our family, though, we don't stay mad for long.

Mom ended up being okay, and we got a break. That was the longest I ever stayed in camp. I was in the wilderness seventeen days straight. We were in for a seven-day hunt, and I think Jeff brought more hunters in for a ten-day hunt. I don't even think my little brother realized I stayed in that long.

Mom, you amaze me and wow me with everything you've done. I look at the different faces of the pictures that you have left behind and none of the faces look the same. They all tell of the life that you have left behind. From the good times to bad times and all the struggles in between. The old house that you lived in where the wind would blow through the cracks in the window and doors. Where we left the water to drip in the sinks so the water wouldn't freeze in the winter. Where the old wood shed was more often empty than full.

Five kids to feed and clothe with very little money to spare. Drive them to school, work around the ranch, and then pick them up again. Jackie would get the new clothes that were very few, and Jerrie would get the left over. The other three children were not sure where they got theirs, but no one will ever know. Seven people in an old wooden house, three bedrooms, one bathroom. We always felt it was from riding up and down the trail in the winter, through the rain and sometimes the snow. She said the cold was finally getting into her bones.

As I pause for a second, then walk over to the picture window and stand there, I can feel the joy she must have felt. Looking out the window, the sun shining on her face as she saw the horses grazing out in the field. Her dogs running around barking really at nothing. The hired hands working down at the barn or out fixing fence. Dave and Les, just to name a few. Then Leon of course, and all the neighbor kids just coming over just to hang out. If you wanted something to eat you fixed it yourself. I guess the Hoeffner's was the place to be. As I listen real close, I can hear the laughter that she must have heard, and I can see the smile that I am sure would appear over her face when she looked out her kitchen window. Our mother loved laughter and she loved the neighbor kids like her own. I find myself smiling more, and maybe even laughing a little whenever I think of our mom.

I can see mom and Jesus having a little tug of war. Mom wanting to stay and get her work done, and Jesus saying "It's time to come home and rest your tired body." I remember Jackie saying mom was digging her heels in a little bit, she wasn't going easy. I think she was tired, she had worked so hard her whole life, not that she didn't have fun. She had a lot of that with all her friends. Taco night, going dancing, spending time with family. I think one of the most relaxing was her bonfire, just sitting outside at night with the fire and the stars up above; the horses close by in the barn, or maybe driving her tractor. I remember a time I told mom I was trying and she said trying doesn't get the job done. That is how she lived her life, getting things done.

We are all so sad she left us, but she has so many people waiting for her at the gate. Our dad, her mom and dad, and her sister JoAnne and her brother in law Dick Klick. Too many others to count. Her two favorite horses and her one crazy dog and a couple of more normal ones, too. She can go for a ride with her dad, and have long talks with her mom and sister. Then she can get caught up with all her friends. Maybe Dave can teach her to rope a grizzly! It's been a long time since she has seen our dad. I think it has been about twenty-six years. That's a long time not to see your partner. It's kind of neat, us kids sent both of them off wearing their cowboy hats and boots.

The one thing the five of us kids know is that she will always stay in our hearts, and her memories will never fade in time. As her children, we will make her proud of us here on earth until the time we can see them both again. So, I guess, that is why the words amazing, strong, proud, and kind describe mom. Most of all mom was beautiful to her five children. One of the last things mom said to me was, "Penny, I love you and always walk tall."

Jeff

Left to right: Colin, Kenny, Jeff, Caitlin, and Marie Hoeffner along the Chinese Wall. Jim Stein taking photo. In 2016, in memory of Mary Faith, Jeff and Marie took their family to the Chinese Wall. Before she passed away, Mary Faith was planning a trip to the Wall with her grandkids, 2016.

Mary Faith Hoeffner was much more than a mother to me. Mom instilled in me a way of life that very few people get to experience anymore. In different ways, my four older sisters and I inherited her love for horses, hunting, ranching, and the mountains.

My father and I were very close. As the only son, I worked by his side in the outfitting business every summer throughout my youth and full time after high school. When dad died in 1989, it hit all of us very hard. But, mom and I made it our mission to make sure the business that dad put his heart and soul into would survive. Mom was a strong-willed woman, and I felt committed to helping her. We struggled through this difficult period, but we made it work until we sold it in 1998.

Mom always had the grit to overcome the many obstacles she faced during her life. She was not afraid to face anything, and I truly believe her love for horses gave her strength to keep going. They were the therapy that kept the most difficult times in her life off her mind. They made her happy! One winter, when dad and I were trucking cattle, she had been down at the barn working with her horses and, instead of walking, she decided to throw a halter on a horse and ride it bareback up to the house. The horse slipped on ice and she broke her leg. No one was home so she had to hobble up to the house and call a friend. She said she'd be ready by spring to go in the mountains, and she was.

Mom was a capable woman. She could do most anything in the backcountry whether wrangling, cooking, guiding hunters, or even leading a pack string. On the ranch, she loved to put up hay, especially driving an open tractor whether swathing, baling, or raking hay. She knew how to drive a team of horses whether putting up hay with a buck rake or pulling a sleigh in the winter.

She loved the mountains.

Mom wasn't afraid of anything... not even bears.

On our traveling trips, she slept under an open fly by the cook stove. A few times, in the middle of the night I'd hear mom hollering my name, "Jeff, I think there's a bear by the camp stove." She never got out of her sleeping bag, just waited until I got the bear out. During hunting camp at Meadow Creek, we had problems with grizzly bears, and mom always slept in the cook tent with the meat coolers on the other side of the canvas tent. One morning, I came down and a grizzly bear had rummaged through the coolers. I asked mom if she had heard anything during the night and she said, "No." Well, a grizzly bear got into the coolers and was a foot from her head.

Left to right: Kevin Gardner (guide), Jeff, Colin, Marie, and Mary Faith Hoeffner, 1994.

When my children were babies, mom didn't want much to do with them. The day they could ride a horse, though, she began paying a lot more attention to them. Colin, my oldest son, made several trips back in the mountains with mom beginning at the age of one. I took him back to hunting camp as a toddler and mom was so proud of her little cowboy. Kenny and Caitlin followed suit. They knew they had to become good horsemen to spend time with grandma. Our most enjoyable trip was when my whole family and our good friends, the Halmeses, took a trip back to our Meadow Creek camp. Mom was in heaven having her three young grandchildren with her. When Kenny and Caitlin were in high school they asked grandma if they could go camping with her at a trailhead on the base of the Continental Divide. She was elated and wanted to take the kids for "a little ride." Seven hours later they returned to camp.

Mom was as tough as they come. The last time I remember mom riding was when we drove our cows off summer pasture in the Elkhorn Mountains to our ranch in Winston. At the age of 82, she rode the whole day with her favorite companion, Toby, a red heeler-corgi. Again, mom never missed a chance at a long day of riding.

She loved her horses so much that when her two favorite horses, Macho and Rooster, were becoming too old to withstand the harsh Lincoln winters, she had a veterinarian put them down. "They're never leaving the ranch," she said. And that made her at peace with her difficult decision.

Mom was the most resilient person I have ever known. She had a real zest for life. After being near death three times, she lived on her own again, drove again, and even made it to the Lincoln rodeo to watch her grandchildren perform. She truly amazed her family and, even more, her doctors. When she was dying and lying by the window, we'd walk the horses by the window and that would bring a smile to her face.

My mom taught me many things, but most of all, she ingrained in all of us a deep appreciation for the simple gifts God gave us: family, horses, and the mountains (maybe not in that order since horses always came first)! Even though mom is gone, her spirit lives through her children and grandchildren who all strive to walk in her footsteps. We sure miss that pickup and horse trailer coming up our road.

Memorial for Mary Faith and Kenneth R. Hoeffner in Hooper Park, Lincoln, Montana. The memorial reads, "In Memory of Kenny and Mary Faith Hoeffner, Wilderness Outfitters, K Lazy Three Ranch of Lincoln."

ABOUT THE COMPILER

Brad Hansen earned a master's degree in environmental history from Utah State University in 2013 and currently works for the Montana Historical Society. In his free time, Brad is a fly fishing guide on Montana's beautiful Missouri River.

The Hoeffner children would like to thank Brad Hansen for all his hard work and the time he put into compiling and completing this book.

Made in the USA
Lexington, KY
30 April 2018